Catherine Carrigan

Experts Confirm This Approach Works

"Catherine Carrigan does a thorough search and identification of the many factors that can cause or contribute to the more common types of depression. I can corroborate her findings based on the many years of research we did at what was the largest psychiatric clinic in New York, the North Nassau Medical Center, where I was the medical doctor for over 25 years."

David R. Hawkins, M.D., Author of *Power Vs. Force: An Anatomy of Consciousness* and Co-Author with Linus Pauling of *Orthomolecular Psychiatry: Treatment of Schizophrenia*

"Catherine's simple and practical approach to healing yourself from depression through nutrition and the body-mind connection helps us to get our lives back on track. This is a much-needed book for everyone who suffers from depression in any form. Thank you, Catherine, for sharing your life with us."

Elizabeth Barhydt, Co-Author, *Self-Help for Stress and Pain* and *Self-Help for Kids: Improving Performance and Building Self-Esteem*

"Catherine Carrigan has opened th⸗ ⸗ ⸗ ⸗ ⸗ ⸗ people who suffer from depression,

D1239302

useful book based on her own experiences with the disease. Catherine has done her research well and includes practical alternatives that everyone can explore to find what works for them. I will recommend the book to my students and clients."

Paul E. Dennison, Ph.D., President, Educational Kinesiology Foundation, and Co-Author, *Brain Gym: Simple Activities for Whole Brain Learning*

"Many people, including health professionals, believe that serious depressions can be treated only by powerful drugs, electroshock and various forms of psychological and behavioral therapies. This book is a personal road map for sufferers that lays out the other routes toward healing. Written by a woman who has been there, this book offers new hope for people who find themselves constantly struggling to attain happiness."

Melvyn R. Werbach, M.D., Author, *Nutritional Influences on Mental Illness: A Sourcebook of Clinical Research*

"The story told by Catherine Carrigan is one of hope, where so many people now suffering don't have hope. It has insights and resources that can make the difference between just being alive and making the commitment to take charge of your life and be your own primary care provider. It will help you be able to utilize the specialists

in the health care field to your own best advantage. Read this book and regain your hope and maybe even your zest for living."
John F. Thie, D.C., Author, *Touch for Health,* and Founding Chairman, International College of Applied Kinesiology

"This is a wonderful book that can really help people who are depressed. This is a book with heart and facts combined. If you're suffering from depression, this book will give you the hope you need and the way out. You'll see a light at the end of your long tunnel."
Jerry V. Teplitz, J.D., Ph.D., Author, *Switched-On Living: Easy Ways to Use the Mind-Body Connection to Energize Your Life*

"Catherine Carrigan's unique book should be read and digested by people with depression and the professionals and families who care for them. Comprehensive, yet concise. Interesting, practical, and timely. It provides readers with an in-depth look at many of the causes of depression and what can be done to overcome them. I highly recommend this book."
William G. Crook, M.D., Author, *The Yeast Connection and Women's Health* and *The Yeast Connection Handbook*

"Catherine Carrigan has written one heart-filled comprehensive book for helping people who suffer from depression. As a body-oriented psychotherapist and muscular therapist, I found her book to be fantastic and a source of hope for mankind. It offers a wealth of useful information for people to incorporate into their lives about how to create wellness. This book is a much-needed, long-overdue guide that I feel will help a great number of people -- those who suffer with depression as well as the psychotherapists who counsel/treat people who suffer from depression. I urge my colleagues to read this book with an open mind, heart, and spirit. You will realize and receive its powerfulness, the holistic approach to healing depression. I recommend this book for both my clients and my colleagues."
Denise Borrelli, Ph.D., L.M.H.C., A.T.R., L.M.T., Director of Education and Massachusetts Chapter President for the American Massage Therapy Association; Adjunct Professor, Springfield College Graduate School of Art Psychotherapy

"Catherine Carrigan explores the causes of depression, understanding that it has different origins in different people and that multiple aspects must be explored to uncover those factors needed for recovery. Her book stands as a holistic self-help manual that the reader can use to begin to understand the chemical origins of depression.

Ms. Carrigan has been through the fires; she has walked the walk and now is ready to talk the talk. Her experiences, both her triumphs and her failures in finding her way back to health, are enlightening and encouraging and give a ray of sunshine for weary travelers with depression to use as a guide in their own quests."

Paul A. Goldberg, M.H.H., D.C., Professor of Clinical Nutrition and Gastroenterology Director, The Goldberg Clinic, Marietta, Georgia

"Catherine Carrigan is one of the strong voices in the world for the holistic treatment of depression. In her book, *Banish the Blues NOW*, Catherine gives the reader a plethora of information on how to recover from depression without having to resort to solely using pharmaceuticals. Her focus on treating the body and the mind as equally important makes this book a necessity for many people who suffer from the debilitating effects of depression."

Paul J. Leslie, Ed.D., Psychotherapist and Author of *Potential Not Pathology: Helping Your Clients Transform Using Ericksonian Psychotherapy*

Banish the Blues

NOW

By Catherine Carrigan

NOW Series Books are available for order through
Ingram Press Catalogues

Catherine Carrigan
Visit my websites at
www.catherinecarrigan.com
www.unlimitedenergynow.com

Printed in the United States of America
First Printing: July 2105
ISBN: 978-0-9894506-0-7

MEDICAL DISCLAIMER

TABLE OF CONTENTS

BOOK II

THE MEDICAL CONNECTION

INTRODUCTION

FOREWORD

If there is a disease more appalling and devastating to patients and their families than depression, I have yet to run across it.

Even schizophrenic patients -- the most tragic sufferers -- suffer excruciatingly when they are depressed.

Unfortunately, those who have not suffered deep depression cannot understand what is going on.

They equate the mood with the occasional moments when they have been sad or have grieved over the loss of something or some relationship.

But there is no comparison.

The great psychoanalyst Dr. Karl Menninger compared this difficulty in grasping the nature of depression to the predicament of a lone fish in a school of fish in the ocean.

That fish has been hooked by a fishing line and is struggling mightily to escape.

None of the other fish can see the line and don't understand why their colleague is so agitated and disturbed.

Many of my patients have told me they would sooner lose an arm than go through another bout of depression.

The only way to really know what depression is like is to have one.

I do not recommend that anyone should do so.

Over 40 years ago I took some adrenochrome as part of our research into the causes of schizophrenia. I suffered a two-week depression with powerful paranoid features.

Only when the depression suddenly lifted did I become aware of what had happened to me. I have never forgotten the experience.

I am therefore very sensitive to the need to have books such as this one appear so that others can benefit by reading about it and not by having to suffer through it on their own.

They will then know what they should do if they should become depressed and will be better at supporting their friends and relatives if they should suffer depression.

But Ms. Carrigan does more than describe her depression. She also outlines in an interesting way what she did for herself with a lot of help from others and provides a guide for other depressed people to follow.

The description of her descent and recovery from her mood disorder is followed by the guide that comprises most of the book. I am pleased by her unusual way of presenting her program.

Listed in the medical connection section are all the physical and physiological factors that can produce deep depression.

Those factors include environmental allergies, which are a common cause of depression.

This statement is as surprising for psychiatrists as it was for me when I first realized the truth of it more than 30 years ago.

I had observed that nearly two-thirds of my depressed patients had histories of allergic reactions going back to their childhoods.

I mentioned this to a colleague who did not believe me.

I challenged him to review his own cases of depression; he did so and confirmed the observation.

How many psychiatrists know that antidepressants started out as antihistamines?

These factors are the substance of orthomolecular psychiatry and have yet to find their way into the medical curricula or their textbooks.

But they are very real and most important. I could not practice psychiatry without attention to these factors.

In this book, stress is honored by a section of its own. Stress by itself may or may not *cause* depression, but when a person is depressed ordinary stressors become intolerable.

A major treatment section details the importance of nutrition and the use of nutrients, vitamins and minerals.

Ms. Carrigan is describing the modern vitamins-as-treatment paradigm in contrast to the outmoded and limited vitamins-as-prevention-only paradigm.

Finally, since there can be no feeling of depression without a mind, she gives proper attention to the mind.

That is not to say that psychotherapy alone or any of its hundreds of different forms, group or individual, have ever been shown to be effective in treating depression.

It is the total program as described in this valuable book that will bring most people out of depression.

Antidepressant drugs will have to be used in many cases, but they are adjuncts to the rest of the program and should be eliminated as soon -- but as carefully -- as possible.

I have become more and more convinced that personal accounts such as this are of the utmost importance in educating people about the ravages of diseases such as depression.

These personal accounts, labeled "anecdotes" by the unthinking, are more helpful than the dry as-dust clinical accounts that still occasionally appear in the psychiatric books.

No course in the understanding or treatment of

depression can be adequate unless this book and other similar books are part of the prescribed reading material.

ABRAM HOFFER, M.D., Ph.D., FRCP(C)

Editor, *The Journal of Orthomolecular Medicine*

Chapter 1: Reflection

"You've got to keep thinking
You can make it thru these waves
Acid, booze, and ass
Needles, guns, and grass
Lots of laughs lots of laughs
Everybody's saying that hell's the hippest way to go
Well I don't think so
But I'm gonna take a look around it though
Blue I love you."
Joni Mitchell

It has now been 18 years since my first book, *Healing Depression: A Holistic Guide,* was first published by Heartsfire Books of Sante Fe, New Mexico.

That book was a labor of love written over a three-year period.

It became the handbook for the Seattle-based Holistic Depression Network, which taught people how to heal their blue funk without drugs.

A few years ago, one of my clients visiting a Los Angeles library found the book translated into Chinese.

I thought, "If I wrote a book good enough to be translated into Chinese, maybe I should try this writing thing again."

I went on to write *What Is Healing? Awaken Your Intuitive Power for Health and Happiness* and *Unlimited Energy Now,* both of which proceeded to become Amazon No. 1 best sellers.

During this time of writing my most recent books, usually once a week, I would hear from people suffering from melancholia or find out about another person who committed suicide, the 10th leading cause of death in the United States.

When I wrote that first book, I was motivated by the thought that if I helped even just one person avoid what I had been through, my efforts would be totally worth it.

I have now been free of psychiatric medication for 22 years.

This is a considerably greater period of time than the 18 years I took lithium and antidepressants.

Despite my best efforts, I wasn't able to feel permanently happy until I started on the path I am now sharing with you.

Why is this timely and relevant?

- The Centers for Disease Control and Prevention reports that 11 percent of all Americans over the age of 12 take antidepressants.

- Women are more likely than men to take these drugs at every level of severity of depression.

- Non-Hispanic white persons are more likely to take antidepressants than are non-Hispanic black and Mexican-American persons.

- Of those taking antidepressants, 60 percent have taken them for more than two years, and 14 percent have taken the drugs for more than 10 years.

- About 8 percent of persons age 12 and over with no current depressive symptoms took antidepressant medication.

- Despite the widespread acceptance of natural healing methods, from 1988-1994 through 2005-2008, the rate of antidepressant use in the United States among all ages increased nearly 400 percent.

It is my prayer that my new book will be of service in providing guidance and solutions.

It's time to update and share the latest wisdom about how you can banish the blues *now.*

Chapter 2: From My Heart to Your Heart

"I find hope in the darkest of days, and focus in the brightest. I do not judge the universe."
Dalai Lama

I am sharing my story because I believe there are literally millions of others who are searching for a better way not just to manage their despondency but to eliminate it finally and entirely.

If you are currently suffering from heavyheartedness, I humbly offer this story to you, and I hold out this hope: You can heal your mind as surely as you can heal a broken leg.

I am not a doctor. I have never been to medical school. I have no training in psychotherapy, psychiatry, counseling or suicide prevention.

What I do have is something I would not now trade for anything: a lifelong experience battling, and at last overcoming, chronic desolation.

For 18 years I took the very best pills, followed the advice of countless well-meaning psychiatrists and spent untold hours talking out the complexities of a difficult life.

Despite the amount of money, time and effort devoted to my mental health, I never knew what it meant to be mentally balanced until I was forced, by ill health, to find this alternative path.

Chapter 3: For Whom Is This Book Written?

*"For I consider that the sufferings of this present time
are not worth comparing with the glory that is to be
revealed to us."*
Romans 8:18

I am writing this book for all who suffer the blues,
whether that cheerlessness be of the short- or long-
term variety.

Although there is a difference between chronic
depression and the short-term varieties, my research has
found that much of what happens in the mind and the
body is the same.

I believe, therefore, that anyone who is depressed, for
whatever reasons, will be able to benefit from this book.

If you have been under the treatment of a conventional
psychiatrist, appreciate what he or she has to offer you,
but do not easily accept the idea that you are doomed to

choose between only two options, drugs or down-heartedness.

Do not easily accept a psychiatric diagnosis until you and your doctors have made a thorough examination to see if your poor spirits may have physical causes, especially if you are in poor health in addition to being depressed.

Chapter 4: My Life of Mental Illness

"In this sad world of ours, sorrow comes to all; and, to the young, it comes with bitterest agony, because it takes them unawares. The older have learned to ever expect it. Perfect relief is not possible, except with time. You cannot now realize that you will ever feel better. Is not this so? And yet it is a mistake. You are sure to be happy again. To know this, which is certainly true, will make you some less miserable now."
Abraham Lincoln

I was hospitalized for manic depression at the age of 20, but that isn't the first time I was ever in serious emotional trouble.

In fact, as I look back over the fabric of my life, I can't detect at what point emotional instability began to unravel the threads that were supposed to hold me together.

Inside myself, I knew there was no logical reason for the

turmoil I experienced on a daily basis. I wished I could be optimistic and just look on the bright side, but frequently there was little logical connection between the severity of my moods and what was or was not happening around me. Other people were always telling me to "cheer up" or "put a smile on your face."

I always wished my solution was so simple.

Once, at Brown University, I remember bursting into tears in the middle of a restaurant while I was having lunch with my two best friends in the whole world.

They were doing their best to love me, to boost me up. I remember it was a beautiful, sunny day, and the two people whom I admired most were telling me what a great writer I was and what a great future I had in store for me.

For some reason, the more my friends talked about my brilliant future, the more terrified I became. Emotion flooded through my body so violently that I could not eat, could not think, could not stop sobbing. I could not imagine the future at all because the present was so terribly frightening.

I didn't know how I could live through the next day, let alone the years to come.

Most days, when I was depressed, I just felt a serious lack of energy and connectedness. On medium-bad days I walked around in a quiet state of desperation. When the heaviness of heart was really bad, well, it was really bad.

On the worst days I hallucinated and heard voices, usually encouraging me to kill myself.

Whether my woefulness was really, really bad, somewhat bad, mildly bad or just kind of bad, I wasn't much fun to be around.

Meanwhile, during these formative years, I went from one state of sickliness to another.

As a little girl, I had constant earaches to the point where I had my ears operated on at age six and my tonsils taken out shortly afterwards.

At seven, I was so allergic to bug bites that I developed scabs all over my legs that had to be washed regularly with antibiotic soap.

Part of my wardrobe had to include a handkerchief because I was seemingly allergic to everything and spent a good part of most days sneezing.

At 15, I became anorexic, dropping to a low of 85 pounds but mostly hovering around 90. Then I flip-flopped to the other extreme. Three years after my low of 85, I weighed about 150.

Being young, without much judgment of my own, around this fat phase I began engaging in sexual activity. So, naturally, I did what so many other college coeds were doing and started taking the Pill. This made my moods much worse, and my crying jags became real emotional upheavals, especially before my period.

To top things off, although I was never much of a drinker, there was alcohol, which only made my blue funk much worse.

And although I was smart enough to avoid hard drugs, which seemed to make even my most stable friends weirder than I could usually handle, I did smoke some marijuana.

Had I been less liberal, I might have had better health.

Psychologists and psychiatrists of various backgrounds and experience levels and with different degrees of caring came into my life and went until I had what's commonly referred to as a nervous breakdown.

In case you've never had the pleasure of having a nervous breakdown, you may not realize that in such a state one doesn't really eat or sleep or have any concept of the passage of time.

It's like being dropped down a well without a rope. There isn't any beginning or end. You don't really know where you are or have any clue how to get out - a very frightening experience.

After my first nervous breakdown, a psychiatrist put me on Valium. I felt drugged and suppressed, yet the feelings of hopelessness and unpredictable days of anxiety continued.

Instinctively, I knew that particular drug was totally wrong for me.

Finally, after two months, I decided to stop taking Valium every day. I got tired of my family asking me, every time I felt depressed, "Did you take your pill?"

Off Valium, I didn't feel much better or much worse, but at least I could think for myself again. I remember driving by my favorite park one summer afternoon and seeing details, such as the light flickering on the leaves, that seemed to have totally escaped me when I was so heavily sedated.

Even after I no longer took Valium every day, I continued to turn occasionally to that little yellow pill out of fear -- whenever I felt really bad.

After all, I didn't know any alternative and was still very much unbalanced. I suffered from a chronically upset stomach, constant colds and yeast infections, and the incessant fear in the back of my mind that I might have another nervous breakdown and lose further touch with time, reality and other people.

Four months later, it came. I was hospitalized after threatening to kill myself.

I remember the mental hospital very well. It was next to a river, not a bad place as these sorts of institutions go, and surrounded by a large wooded area where I was able to take long walks once the doctors determined I was an acceptable risk.

Although the people there were all well-intentioned, I still shudder when I think of the place. The whole memory seems slightly blurred, like an old motion picture that has been slowed down and faded out. Were it any sharper, it might hurt too much.

Of course, at the time, no one bothered to ask whether my crazy college diet or the fact that I had a yeast infection might be contributing to my suicidal desperation.

During my research in later years, I spoke with Dr. William Crook, the author of *The Yeast Connection* books.

He told me about a patient who had been able to get out of a mental hospital after going on a yeast-free diet.

What would my life have been like if I had known then what I know now?

I might have avoided the psychiatric label, might have been able to avoid so much shame and most of all might have avoided untold thousands of dollars spent on psychiatric bills and an immeasurable amount of abject suffering.

Maybe I wasn't ready for this approach, as I was when I got sick in my late thirties. I am grateful that I found it at all, frankly, and that the rest of my life will be almost indescribably better.

One thing was certain, though: When I went into the mental hospital in 1981, drugs were the most important solution, and nutrition wasn't even discussed.

That first night in the mental hospital, the nurses gave me new medications in a paper cup.

When I woke up the next morning, my vision was so blurry I could barely see across the room.

Perhaps that's why my memories of that place are fuzzy.

I was so dizzy I could hardly stand up. I later learned I had been placed on lithium and antidepressants.

It was there, in the mental hospital, that the psychiatrist who admitted me told me I was manic-depressive. I didn't really know what that meant, but the way he told me, it seemed like I was a very bad person who should be very ashamed of herself.

After 10 days of incarceration, I vowed I would never put myself in the position of being hospitalized again, no matter how bad I felt.

In the years that followed, although I continued to suffer so excruciatingly that at times I could think of little else but suicide, I survived -- which is partly my point.

Truthfully, I cannot tell you that I believe psychiatric medications serve no purpose. I believe most doctors who prescribe them and most patients who take them are acting in good faith. They think they are following the best solution, often responding to what feels like a crisis situation.

At first the drugs did manage to give me a more even temperament. I was very grateful for them. I was so grateful for lithium, in fact, that I was afraid I wouldn't be able to live a day without it. I followed my doctor's protocols to the letter.

I never missed a pill because I was terrified of what would happen if I missed even a single dose. Every major event in my life – the job changes, moves to new cities, insurance changes, even the marriage that brought me to Atlanta – was carefully choreographed so I would never be without my lithium or antidepressants.

Yet during all those 18 years of medication - 15 on lithium and antidepressants, three on various other psychiatric drugs - and endless psychotherapy, I continued to face, on a more or less regular and repeated basis, times when I could think of little else but suicide.

At those times, I was terrified not just of the blues but of myself.

I was terrified that some uncontrollable element of my nature would again rise up and cause me the pain and humiliation I remembered from my hospitalization.

Not to mention the worry. I had so much to worry about.

Would I ever be able to pass myself off as "normal"?

There was always someone - a new in-law, a new friend, even old friends - who eventually discovered a scarlet letter, that I was taking psychiatric medication. I discovered many people were ready to snub me for suffering from an illness they didn't understand.

When I married, I worried whether I'd pass on my disease to any children I might conceive - if I could even have one.

I worried about the chance that a fetus conceived while I was taking lithium might develop a fatal heart defect. And, I had to wonder, would I outlive the usefulness of my lithium?

There were few long-term studies, at least none anyone wanted to discuss with me. The doctors sometimes did check my blood levels and monitor my side effects, asking me vague questions about kidney function and my thyroid gland.

No one could tell me what lithium might eventually do to my kidneys. Every time I passed a dialysis center, I wondered if I might end up inside.

Most of all, I was ashamed of not being able to lick my illness.

When I was fat, I could lose weight. If I had been an alcoholic or a drug addict, I could have conquered my addiction.

For most of my life, however, there seemed to be no way to overcome my particular brand of affliction.

It didn't matter how many biographies I read of famous artists or beloved writers or movie stars who suffered the same way.

Friends sometimes speculated that my ability to write was the gift behind my instability, as if I couldn't be creative unless I was also mentally ill.

My standard reply: "It's not worth it. Nothing is worth this much suffering."

I felt like the condemned man in the Greek myth, fated to forever keep rolling the rock up the hill, only to have it roll back and flatten me, time after time.

Sometimes an unpleasant life event would coincide with the bad moods, and sometimes I could find no logical reason for having gone off the deep end.

I got very tired of being repeatedly flattened by that heavy stone, no matter how carefully I choreographed my life or how scrupulously I followed each doctor's exact instructions.

I excelled at my schoolwork, at various jobs as a newspaper reporter, and as a fledgling playwright, and yet there was always my mental illness to humble me to the last degree.

Chapter 5: The Climb Out of Darkness

"Nothing ever goes away until it has taught us
what we need to know."
Pema Chodron

I have now been totally off all psychiatric medication for 22 years with no relapse.

Most patients who relapse do so within five months or less.

And in my former life as a mentally ill person, I had what the psychiatrists called "episodes" at least four times a year, especially around the changing of the seasons and of course during those all-star stress marathons, Christmas and Thanksgiving.

I began the actual process of withdrawing from the medication in October 1994, and with each decrease in dosage, my physical symptoms dramatically improved.

From the beginning of my withdrawal from the

medication, the importance of the alternative approach I was taking did not escape me.

I figured that if what I was doing worked for me – and I was the one who suffered so excruciatingly – it would certainly work for many other people if they only knew what to do.

If you were here with me now, as we conclude this introduction, I might give you a hug and take you on a tour of my garden on your way back home.

If it were spring or summer or even fall, there would be some glory of nature to appreciate - a bluebird nesting in the box behind my backyard hammock or perhaps a flush of daisies washing over the bank of my hillside. Even in winter, without flowers, there is a texture and a richness to nature, a boundless wisdom in the way the humblest leaf is put together.

Even in the midst of despair, there is beauty to enrich the spirit and an intelligence that directs our most unconscious drive for life.

It is all here for your benefit.

BOOK I

Get Started

.

Chapter 1: Develop Trusting Relationship With Whole Body Health Care Provider

"The underlying concept remains that the majority of behavioral problems do not arise from organic causes but rather from an assortment of conflicts, hostilities, guilt, dependencies, personality immaturities and so forth. This bias toward philosophical causes has created a situation in which the majority of behavioral problems are not seriously subjected to a differential diagnosis based on a full range of organic causes." William H. Philpott and Dwight Kalita

There we have the beginning of the problem: Each of us is a collection of neuroses, repressed memories, masks and dreams.

The blues, when it appears, looks like a purely mental disease.

On the surface, its causes appear to be rooted in childhood

and the victim's philosophical attitude and current state of personal crisis.

Maybe you can look at your life and conclude that your heaviness of heart is a logical outcome of your present circumstances. Even if that's the case, you may do well to read on.

Depression is a complex disease involving virtually every organ and energy system in our body. It may be genetic. It may have been caused by a virus, as many researchers currently believe. It may begin with faulty digestion or an imbalance in the brain structures that regulate hormones and emotions.

It may be caused by an inability to regulate blood sugar or to metabolize carbohydrates or protein. It may be the result of an allergic reaction. It may happen when delicate brain mechanisms are exposed to a toxic chemical.

But even when it occurs as a response to a sudden stressful life event, it changes our body chemistry.

If you are known to have a psychiatric diagnosis, it will be much easier for your medical doctor to brush off your physical complaints as psychosomatic, dash off a prescription for an antidepressant and hurry off to a patient he or she feels has a "real" problem.

It will take a very special health care professional to spend the time to figure out the precise factors contributing to your desolation, be they physical or emotional in nature.

Whatever path brings you here, whether it's a long road or a short one, it's up to you to find a good health care professional who meets the following criteria:

1. You can talk comfortably with him or her.
2. He or she is willing to answer your questions, take you seriously and not brush you off. Your physician should be someone who respects your questions.
3. Most important, that person should be capable of treating the entire mind and body and not be just a specialist in one area.
4. A recent study of doctors who prescribed antidepressants suggests you may be more likely to get to the bottom of the physical factors contributing to your blue funk if you visit a primary care physician.

Primary care physicians diagnose physical disorders -- *i.e.*, nonmental f a c t o r s -- in a majority of the visits in which a depressive disorder is also diagnosed.

On the other hand, if you visit a psychiatrist, the chances of medical, nonmental factors being discovered may be less than one in 10.

Why is your choice of doctor so important? Because if your partner in recovery misses crucial clues that might lead to uncovering the real source of your desperation, you may end up suffering even more.

In *Toxic Psychiatry,* a book critical of his own profession, Dr. Peter Breggin writes:

"If a psychiatrist is faced by a depression that is genuinely hormonal or biochemical in origin, the worst thing he can do is to give the patient psychiatric medications, all of which worsen the biochemical condition of the brain."

Chapter 2: Start Making Connections

"The balance of our very physiological well-being depends intimately not only on its innate condition but also on all the external reality surrounding it, up to and including the forces of the macrocosm."
John C. Pierrakos

Once you have found a health care professional or team of doctors who can coordinate your care, you must provide them with accurate, precise information about which factors seem to influence your moods most predominantly.

Get a notebook and begin to track how the following variables affect your state of mind:

1. What you ate at each meal
2. Time of each meal
3. Snacks
4. What you drank with and between meals
5. Moods throughout the day

6. Any physical symptoms, whether or not they seem related to your mental well-being
7. Menstrual cycles
8. Weather
9. Number of hours you slept at night
10. Number of naps
11. Any medications you took that day
12. Amount of alcohol consumed
13. Number of cigarettes smoked
14. Kind of exercise and amount of time spent exercising
15. Important events in your emotional life and how you reacted to them
16. Overall ranking of how you felt in body and mind
17. Any other factors that seemed to have had an impact on how you felt emotionally or physically
18. Optional, if a thyroid condition is suspected: Underarm body temperature (see Book II, Chapter 6).

In addition to helping your doctors find patterns so they can treat you more effectively, this information may be the greatest tool you have to persuade yourself to follow a healthier lifestyle.

Several companies publish health diaries, but any simple notebook will suffice.

If you choose to follow an elimination diet (see Book II, Chapter 15) keep accurate records of that process in your diary, too.

Chapter 3: You Deserve to Feel Good

"I can't change the world but I can change
the world in me."
Paul David Hewson, a.k.a. Bono

Write down your level of agreement with the following statements.

If you totally agree, mark "100 percent."

If you feel ambivalent, note on a percentage basis how much you agree or disagree.

I deserve to be happy. I am ___ percent positive about this. I am ___ negative about this.

I deserve to be physically healthy. I am ___ percent positive about this. I am ___ negative about this.

I am guided by a higher power that has my best interests in mind. I am ___ percent positive about this.

I am ___ percent negative about this.

Before you can get well, you must be motivated to do so. If you find that you have any negative beliefs here, ask yourself if you are ready to let them go.

Chapter 4: Let the Good Times Roll

*"The more energy we let flow, the healthier we are.
Illness in the system is caused by an imbalance of energy
or a blocking of the flow of energy."*
Barbara Ann Brennan

Ask yourself to what extent you agree with the following statements:

I deserve the best in life.

I am worthy of love just the way I am.

I love myself unconditionally.

I love others unconditionally.

I deserve ___.

I need to forgive ___.

If only I could forget ___ I could be happy now.

If only I had ___ I could be happy now.

There are no right or wrong answers, only a process that will allow you to observe your own thought process.

Joy doesn't require special equipment. You already have a heart and a mind. As you unblock your hidden pain, you will bring yourself and everyone around you to a higher state of bliss than you ever thought possible.

Chapter 5: Write Your Heart Out

"She stood in the storm, and when the wind did not blow her way, she adjusted her sails."
Elizabeth Edwards

When you've experienced stress or trauma, it's important to recognize you have to process the resulting feelings.

If you don't let go of the feelings, the energy of all those emotions gets stored someplace in your body, disrupting the health of your internal organs, unbalancing your brain chemistry and generally making you feel miserable.

Much scientific research has been done about the value of journaling.

Even if you never share your story with anyone else, if you put it on paper, it's beginning to work its way out of your system, and you will start to feel better.

Here's how to begin:

1. Get a notebook. It can be as simple as a spiral-bound notebook. This will be the repository of feelings you choose to release through your writing. It's now a sacred document and a major tool for your personal healing.

2. Even if you don't consider yourself to be a writer, give yourself permission to put down on paper what has happened to make you so upset.

3. As you write about what happened, take note of how you are feeling. Connect to the feelings as you write. Feel yourself releasing the stress and trauma with every new word you write.

4. Once your journal is full, burn it. You will be surprised how burning the journal -- which seems almost blasphemous after you've taken the time to fill its pages with your deepest thoughts -- releases even more layers of energy. Give yourself permission to throw it in the fireplace, tearing out the pages one by one and letting the experiences go completely.

Chapter 6: Raise Your Vibration

"Smell the sea, and feel the sky.
Let your soul and spirit fly."
Van Morrison

In terms of pure energy, we know downheartedness; melancholia, sorrow and grief all feel very heavy.

If you are living with these feelings, you probably feel tired a lot and have trouble accomplishing even basic tasks at times.

Looking at this from a pure energy perspective, we have to recognize that all illness is simply slowed-down vibration, and the blues really slow us down to almost an immediate halt.

So if the blues is really just slowed-down energy, we can shift out of this despondent feeling by simply raising our vibration.

How do you raise your vibration?

1. Always have a fool-proof thought. This is a thought that will make you feel happy no matter what. For me, it's the thought of hugging my dog. No matter how bad I feel, if I think of hugging my rescue girl Belle, I know I can feel better. This is an internal state and the place where you begin to feel better.

2. Surround yourself with love and light. Place yourself in the most loving environment possible. Environment is the most powerful factor. Even if you don't feel good, if you surround yourself with loving people and actual sunshine, you will notice yourself starting to feel better.

3. Say a prayer of gratitude. Even when life feels totally desolate, if we give thanks for all we have, all we have experienced and the people around us, we can shift out of the vibration of despondency and start to feel better.

4. Make feeling good your priority. When you make it your priority to feel as good as possible on any given day no matter what, you shift your personal energy.

Sometimes the best you can get to is neutral, but neutral will be better than crying all day, doing nothing or staring at the wall. Ask yourself what you would need to be, do or have today in order to feel better.

5. Give yourself permission to feel good, knowing that whatever you do to raise your own vibration will benefit everybody around you.

What could you do right now, right away, to feel even just a little bit better?

BOOK II

The Medical Connection

Chapter 1: Put On Your Sherlock Holmes Detective Hat

"Psychiatric symptoms may be caused by alcohol-related syndromes, degenerative brain diseases, endocrinopathies, traumatic brain damage, collagen diseases, demyelinating brain diseases, seizures, encephalitides, and toxic and metabolic diseases."
Irl Extein and Mark S. Gold

A number of physical ailments have been positively correlated with the blues. These physical problems may include but are by no means limited to:

Candida or yeast infection
Hypoglycemia
Thyroid problems and other endocrine disorders
(R e c e n t studies suggest that thyroid disorders are the most common physical illnesses contributing to depression while other reported cases suggest that treatment of subclinical hypothyroidism may be all that's necessary to cure life-long ennui)

Environmental allergies and food allergies

Amino acid deficiencies

Electrolyte imbalances

Vitamin or mineral deficiencies

Toxic exposure to heavy metals or chemicals

Cardiopulmonary obstructive disease

Brain tumors

Head injuries

Alzheimer's disease

Strokes and seizures

Hypertension

Viral infections

Diabetes

Insulin resistance or difficulty metabolizing carbohydrates

I cannot overemphasize the importance of this step. What I'm really recommending here is to look deeply and see why your biochemistry is out of balance.

In one study of 250 inpatients of a psychiatric service, for example, 12 percent were found to be suffering from physical conditions that were a causative factor for their emotional illness.

Doctors who care enough to look often find real, identifiable physical illnesses behind their patients' mental suffering.

Chapter 2: Look Up Drug Side Effects

"Most medications prescribed in clinical practice are capable of adversely affecting the central nervous system and producing significant changes in the patient's mood, perception, thinking, cognition, and behavior."

Ghazi Asaad

Before rushing off to find a drug to cure your bleakness, better look in your medicine cabinet to see if any drugs you are already taking for other ailments may be making you depressed.

Medications for a wide variety of physical diseases have been found to cause unhappiness. For example, hypertension was the most commonly coded medical diagnosis found in a recent study of primary care doctors who diagnosed patients with depression.

One of the best websites for this purpose is www.epocrates.com because it allows you to check not only side effects but also how all the medications you are taking interact with each other.

Many times it is not only the side effects of one drug but the sum total of interactions that may be making you feel unwell.

Ironically, many antihypertensive medications, including clonidine, and other agents for treating heart disease such as propranolol, procainamide, hydralazine, reserpine and methyldopa have long been reported to cause melancholia.

The following chart lists other medications that may cause the blues along with other possible side effects:

Anesthetic Medications
Halothane: Anger, tension, fatigue
Isoflurane: Anger, tension, fatigue

Antibiotic Medications
Isoniazid: Auditory and visual hallucinations, catatonia
Cycloserine: Nervousness, irritability, anxiety

Anticancer Medications
Steroids

Decarbazine

Hexamethylamine

Vincristine

Vinblastine: Anxiety

Asparaginase: Personality changes

AntiParkinsonian Agents
Hallucinations, paranoid delusions

Levodopa

Carbidopa

Amantadine

Bromocriptine

Cardiovascular Agents
Propranolol

Procainamide

Reserpine

Methyldopa

Hydralazine

Central Stimulants
Hallucinations, paranoid delusions, insomnia

Ritalin

Amphetamines

Pemoline

Hormone Replacements

Premarin: Headaches, dizziness

Provera: Insomnia

Non-Steroidal Anti-Inflammatory Medications

Indomethacin: Anxiety, agitation, hostility, depersonalization

Sulindac: Anger, combativeness, homicidal feelings, obsessive talking

Over-the-Counter Medications

Phenylpropanolamine

Antihistamines and decongestants

Ephedrine

Pseudephedrine

Aminophylline

Indocin

Corticosteroids

Psychiatric Medications

Antipsychotics: Oversedation, total muteness, malignant syndrome

Lithium

Sedative-Hypnotics: Oversedation, disinhibition

Disuliram: Anxiety

Sources: Irl Extein and Mark S. Gold eds., *Medical Mimics of Psychiatric Disorders;* Ghazi Asaad, *Understanding Mental Disorders Due To Medical Conditions or Substance Abuse;* Ronald Arky, ed., *Physician's Desk Reference*

Chapter 3: It's OK to Take Small Steps

"Blackbird singing in the dead of night, take these broken wings and learn to fly. All your life you were only waiting for this moment to arise."
Paul McCartney and John Lennon

When we're feeling blue, the thought of becoming happy again may feel completely out of reach.

The thought of then researching the various medical factors on top of understanding the way we feel may sound totally impractical because we can barely get through the day.

Remember, you don't have to figure everything out all at once.

Here's how to break that pattern of overwhelm: Give yourself permission to do just one thing every day that might possibly make you 2 percent happier. Just a smidge.

If you feel totally suicidal, beyond all hope, don't try to

solve the whole mess all at once. Just ask yourself what one thing you can be, do, or have that might make you 2 percent better.

Small steps could include:

Taking a hot bath

Calling a friend you haven't heard from in a while

Eating something really yummy

Watching the sunset or sunrise

Taking a nap

Letting yourself break down and cry

If you have been crying for a while, breaking the cycle by getting up and doing something else, even if it is tidying your room

Saying a prayer

Giving yourself a big hug

Walking around the block

Telling someone how you really feel

Going back to church, the synagogue, mosque, meditation group or other spiritual organization you haven't visited for a while

Writing a letter to an old friend

Donating money to a group you really care about

Looking up to the sky and saying "thank you"

Blessing your meal and giving thanks for all you receive

Chapter 4: Forgive Yourself and All Others

"People are often unreasonable and self-centered, forgive them anyway. If you are kind, people may accuse you of ulterior motives, be kind anyway. If you are honest, people may cheat you, be honest anyway. If you find happiness, people may be jealous, be happy anyway. The job you do today may be forgotten, do good anyway. Give the world your best and it may never be enough, give your best anyway. For you see, in the end it is between you and God.
It was never between you and them anyway."
Mother Theresa

As you begin to investigate what's really been going on with your mind-body connection, you may find yourself feeling intense anger, confusion, resentment and regret.

"If only this could have been figured out much sooner," you may think.

Personally, I was on lithium and antidepressants for 18

years. I bore the judgment of many people about my character before sorting through the multiple medical factors that affected the way I felt.

Maybe you have felt miserable even longer. Even a lifetime!

Many people think that if we forgive another person, we are letting them off the hook. In truth, when we forgive others, we are letting ourselves off the hook and reclaiming layers of our old energy.

On the other hand, if we don't forgive, our energy gets stuck in the past.

We become mired down by what could/should have happened according to our own way of thinking.

When your energy is stuck in the past like this, you feel exhausted. You have little vitality left for the life you still have to experience ahead of you.

You may need to forgive yourself for not having known this information before, not having been motivated to get a better handle on things, taking psychiatric medication, whatever!

You may need to forgive the people who tried to help you, whether they were psychologists, psychiatrists, medical doctors who missed what was really going on, your family or people who pushed you to take drugs that didn't make you feel good.

I recommend a simple forgiveness mantra:

I FORGIVE (NAME OF PERSON, GROUP OR ORGANIZATION).

(NAME OF PERSON, GROUP OR ORGANIZATION) FORGIVES ME.

I LOVE (NAME OF PERSON, GROUP OR ORGANIZATION).

(NAME OF PERSON, GROUP OR ORGANIZATION) LOVES ME.

Repeat this mantra until you feel the energy between you and the person or group has shifted.

You may need to say the mantra daily until all the bitterness is gone.

You will know you are completely done with forgiveness when you can think of the person, group or organization with no negative emotional reaction whatsoever.

You are on your path, you are figuring it out!

Keep forgiving yourself and keep going.

I also like:

I FORGIVE MYSELF.

I FORGIVE ALL PAST EXPERIENCE.

I AM FREE!

Chapter 5: Why We as a Society Need to Get Serious About Natural Healing

"What is to give light must endure burning."
Viktor Frankl

We as a society need to get serious about natural healing.

Why?

Of the top 10 drugs known to cause violence, eight are psychiatric drugs, including five highly popular antidepressants, two for learning disabilities and one for insomnia.

Drug overdose was the leading cause of death by injuries in 2010. About 60 percent of those overdoses were from pharmaceuticals. Drug overdoses cause more deaths than traffic accidents.

Over 50 percent of Americans take two prescription drugs, and 20 percent of Americans are on at least five prescription medications.

The average prescription medication has 70 possible adverse side effects, with some posing as many as 525 possible reactions.

Meanwhile, here are the statistics about deaths from natural healing remedies:

1. Deaths from nutritional supplements in the U.S. in 2010: zero.

2. Deaths from yoga in the United States in 2012: I could just find one weird case at a mysterious retreat.

3. Deaths from meditation in the U.S. in 2012: One, see above.

4. Deaths from tai chi: Apparently the rocker Lou Reed was practicing tai chi when he died, but liver disease was listed as his official cause of death.

5. Deaths from flower essences: Although flower essences are used to aid pain and suffering in hospice care, I could find no known deaths that they caused.

The next time someone challenges you for taking a holistic approach to banish your blues, refer back to these statistics.

It simply makes more sense when you do the research.

Who doesn't want to stay safe while getting well?

Chapter 6: Check Your Thyroid

"Thyroid dysfunction is by far the most likely condition to present as depression to the psychiatrist."
Irl Extern and Mark S. Gold

Many People think that depression is simply a phenomenon of the mind.

More accurately, it is a whole-body experience.

One of the first places you will want to look to banish your blues for good is your thyroid, as low thyroid functions will make you feel lethargic and depressed.

SYMPTOMS OF HYPOTHYROIDISM

Physical Symptoms
Hair loss
Yellow-orange discoloration of skin, particularly on the palms of hands
Excess weight
Muscle weakness
Dry skin
Intolerance to cold
Recurrent infections
Drooping, swollen eyes
Constipation

Mental Symptoms
Depression
Fatigue
Loss of appetite

Sources: M. Sara Rosenthal, *The Thyroid Sourcebook*; and W.M.G. Tunbridge, *Thyroid Disease: The Facts.*

Ask your doctor about tests to see if your thyroid level is in the normal range, but be persistent if the results look normal and you still don't feel well.

Experts who have studied the link between depression and thyroid abnormalities say that some people are simply acutely sensitive to thyroid imbalances and that routine testing may identify only about 10 percent of these patients.

The blues may simply be the first sign of hypothyroidism.

Aside from the blood tests your doctor may order to check the levels of thyroid hormones, you can perform a simple underarm temperature test.

Get a basal body temperature thermometer, the kind that is well-calibrated, the kind used to track body temperature for ovulation.

Instead of placing the thermometer in your mouth, put it under your arm first thing in the morning before you get out of bed and keep it there for 10 minutes.

For women, start your measurements on the second day of

menstruation.

If you take your temperature in the middle of your cycle, your results may be skewed when your temperature rises during ovulation. Keep the record for at least five days.

If your underarm temperature is consistently below 97.4 degrees, you may have a problem with low thyroid function.

Chapter 7: Check Your Amino Acids

"A deficiency in amino acids may cause you to feel sluggish, foggy, unfocused and depressed."
Therese Borchard

Amino acids have been used for years to treat the blues with great effectiveness.

Amino acids are not only the building blocks of protein but also the key ingredients for your neurotransmitters - the chemical messengers your brain uses to communicate with nerve cells throughout the body.

Ask your doctor to perform blood tests to check your individual levels as your deficiencies will be unique to your body.

Without the amino acids phenylalanine and tyrosine, for example, your brain can't make the adrenaline or noradrenaline you need to respond to stress.

Recent research has turned up important trends in

amino acid absorption for patients with both depression and manic depression.

One study of patients with major depression, for example, found levels of five large neutral amino acids - tyrosine, phenylalanine, leucine, isoleucine, and valine - to be significantly lower than the levels found in normal individuals.

Another study of people with manic depression found possible abnormalities in the metabolism of tryptophan and tyrosine and that these levels remained unchanged even when patients were being treated for their illness with lithium.

Perhaps the most exciting recent discovery involved gamma aminobutyric acid (GABA), a supposedly nonessential amino acid formed from glutamic acid. Amino acids are classified as essential if the body can't manufacture them on its own.

Taken with the B vitamins niacinamide and inositol, GABA prevents anxiety messages from reaching the brain's motor centers. In simple terms, GABA acts as a tranquilizer.

One study found GABA levels were significantly lower in about one-third of patients with major depression and also low in patients with mania and those with manic depression who were depressed.

In addition, low levels of GABA may be a common inherited trait in families with mood disorders, which has led to speculation that testing for low levels of GABA could show who might be vulnerable to developing mood disorders.

Although tryptophan is the building block for serotonin, low levels of which have been found to be a biochemical predictor of likelihood to commit suicide, the U.S. Food and Drug Administration took it off the market in 1989 because certain individuals developed massive toxic reactions.

In massive doses, tryptophan can cause undesirable perceptual and mood changes. However, it can be absorbed in moderate amounts from food, the best sources of which include pineapple, turkey, chicken, yogurt, bananas and unripened cheese.

According to Dr. Priscilla Slagle, author of *The Way Up From Down,* other alternatives to tryptophan supplementation include magnesium, a mineral that promotes relaxation, and the amino acids taurine and glycine, which calm the nervous system, as well as the B vitamins niacin and niacinamide.

Robert Erdman, author of *The Amino Revolution,* argues that DLPA, a depression-fighting mixture that contains two forms of phenylalanine, is the most effective amino acid for treating the blues because it prevents the breakdown of endorphins, the body's natural painkillers.

Chapter 8: Check Environmental Allergies

"When a person is exposed on an infrequent basis to some substance and has an immediate reaction to that substance, then the cause and effect of the allergy is apparent to all.... When the exposure to an allergy-causing substance is constant, however, eventually the acute symptoms will give way to either a period of no symptoms or to chronic symptoms such as headaches, depression, or arthritis. In other words the acute symptoms have been suppressed because of the constant nature of the exposure and the body has reacted by attempting to adapt itself to the problem."
Theron G. Randolph and Ralph W. Moss

If your food, mood and weather diary indicates that your sadness deepens in the spring or fall or is worse at various times of the day, your moods may well be affected by environmental allergies.

Allergies are traditionally defined by a kind of specific

response the body produces to the presence of an allergen, which can be any substance recognized as a foreign invader.

In this traditional model, the immune system produces antibodies to the allergen. The antibodies attach themselves to mast cells, which release histamine, a chemical that causes tearing, itching and runny noses.

The trouble is that the mast cells that release histamine aren't just located in our noses. They also are located in the brain, and the peripheral neural structures are rich in mast cells.

Histamine is also a neurotransmitter, a chemical that the central nervous system uses to send messages back and forth to the brain. It has been described as an inhibitory neurotransmitter and has been found in extremely high levels in the body chemistry of mental patients who are suicidally depressed.

So when you have an allergic reaction, not only does your nose know it, but your brain feels the effects as well.

Recent research suggests that the immune systems of

some depressed subjects reflect an ongoing inflammatory process throughout the body, complete with higher activation of killer immune cells, both during and after remission.

Doesn't it follow that people who are hypersensitive are allergic to life? That seems to match up with most people's definitions of the word "crazy."

PSYCHOLOGICAL PROBLEMS THAT MAY BE CAUSED BY ALLERGIES

Headaches
Migraine
Vascular
Histamine
Tension
Muscle spasm

Cerebral Depression
Acute and chronic depression
Drowsiness approaching narcolepsy
Episodic dullness or dreaminess
Learning disorders
Tension-fatigue syndrome
Minimal brain dysfunction

Cerebral Stimulation

Restlessness

Nervousness

Anxious, inner shaky feeling

Insomnia

Hyperactivity

Behavior problems

Inappropriate emotional outbursts

Uncontrolled anger

Fear, panic

Psychiatric

Feelings of apartness, spacey

Floating sensation

Episodic amnesia

Pathologically poor memory

Inability to concentrate

Personality changes

Psychoses

Schizophrenia

Autism

Hallucinations

Source: Marshall Mandell and Lynne Waller Scanlon, *Dr. Mandell's 5-Day Allergy Relief System*

Make a list:

My known allergies

My suspected allergies

Symptoms I have that may be associated with allergies

Notice whether your symptoms vary with factors such as the climate, weather, seasons or even locations.

Take note of whether you feel different in your home or office or your garden. Take the notes to your doctor and ask about allergy testing. If you decide to be tested for allergies, make note of any psychological changes that occur during the process.

Chapter 9: Rule Out Toxic Chemicals

"A person suffering from depression is given counseling and medication, but rarely does anyone think to see if that person is being exposed to 1 of the 40 chemicals known to cause depression."
Cynthia Wilson

In the emerging field of environmental illness, it is now generally recognized that such common activities as driving down a modern interstate choked with gas fumes may induce a state of t h e b l u e s. Everything depends of course on t h e relative strength of your immune s y s t e m a n d degree of sensitivity to chemicals as well as the combined total of toxic substances you are exposed to at any given point in time.

Once you recognize that chemicals may be affecting your nervous system, you will be ready to embrace a more organic lifestyle, eliminating toxins in your personal care products, home cleaning supplies and overall environment.

Chemicals that have been observed to cause depression of
the central nervous system include:

Acetaldehyde
Acetylene tetrabromide
sec-Amyl acetate
Benzene
Benzyl alcohol
Benzyl chloride
2-Butoxyethanol
n-Butyl acetate
sec-Butyl acetate
tert-Butyl acetate
Camphor
Carbon tetrachloride
Chlorobenzene
Chloroform
beta-Chloroprene
Cumene
Cyclohexane
Diacetone alcohol
1,1-Dichloroethane
1,2-Dichloroethylene
Dichloromonofluoromethane
2,4 Dichlorophenol

Dichlorotetrafluoroethane

Dimethylaniline

Dinitrotoluenes

2-Ethoxyethyl acetate

Ethyl benzene

Ethyl bromide

Ethyl chloride

Ethyl ether

Ethyl formate

Ethyl mercaptan

Ethyl silicate

Ethylene dichloride

Ethylene glycol

Ethylene glycol dinitrate

Formaldehyde

Formic acid

n-Hexane

Hexone

Hydrazine

Isoamyl acetate

Methyl iodide

Methyl methacrylate

alpha-Methylstyrene

Methylal

Nicotine

Nitromethane
Octane
n-Pentane Propane
n-Propyl alcohol
Isobutyl alcohol
Isophorone
Isopropyl acetate
Isopropyl alcohol
Isopropyl ether
Linalyl alcohol
Mesityl oxide
Methyl n-amyl ketone
Methyl alcohol
Methyl chloride
Methyl formate
Propylene oxide
Pyridine
Styrene
Sulfuryl fluoride
1,1,2,2-Tetrachloroethane
Toluene
1,1,1-Trichloroethane
1,1,2-Trichloroethane
Trichloroethylene
1,2,3 - Trichloropropane

Source: Cynthia Wilson, *Chemical Exposure and Human Health: A Reference to 314 Chemicals With a Guide to Symptoms and a Directory of Organizations*

While many of these chemicals may sound foreign or strange, you may recognize some of them as common ingredients in tobacco smoke, gas, fumes, pesticides, perfumes and many cleaning products you are exposed to on a regular basis.

If you recognize you have chemical toxicity, consult with your doctor, naturopath or nutritionist and make a plan to detoxify your body safely.

Chapter 10: Rule Out Toxic Metals

"Some people have spoken to psychiatrists for years
with little visible progress.
After amalgam removal (of mercury tooth fillings),
they are far more capable of addressing and processing
their problems to completion."
Hal A. Huggins

Historians have theorized that one of the reasons the Roman Empire declined was as a result of contamination from lead pipes.

A hundred years from now, historians may reckon that one of the reasons the blues increased so rapidly in our society was as a result of widespread exposure to toxic metals.

Few of us ever consider the quantity of potentially toxic metals with which we come into contact on a daily basis. Toxic metals are in the fillings in our teeth, in the aluminum pots in which we cook, and in the city water we drink.

We can be exposed to toxic metals in our workplace, in household and gardening chemicals, in cosmetics and even in medications.

In their book *Brain Allergies: The Psychonutrient and Magnetic Connections,* Drs. William H. Philpott and Dwight K. Kalita described heavy metal toxicity as one of the key elements to be considered in diagnosing mental problems, along with nutritional deficiencies or excesses, reactions to foods, chemicals, inhalants, microorganisms and their toxins and finally what they called "learned responses to life experiences."

Heavy metals also are associated with a wide range of physical ailments. Here are some key metals to ask your doctor about and the mental symptoms associated with toxic buildup from each:

Aluminum: Depression, dementia, suicidal thoughts, Alzheimer's disease

Bismuth: Difficulty with memory, hallucinations

Mercury: Depression, psychotic behavior sometimes diagnosed as schizophrenia

Cadmium: Increased sensitivity to pain

Lead: Hyperactivity, fatigue, psychotic behavior sometimes diagnosed as schizophrenia

Copper: Hyperactivity, depression, postpartum psychosis, dementia, autism, PMS, insomnia, senility

Sources: Hal A. Huggins, *It's All in Your Head: The Link Between Mercury Amalgams and Illness;* H. Richard Casdorph and Morton Walker, *Toxic Metal Syndrome: How Metal Poisonings Can Affect Your Brain;* Pat Lazarus, *Healing the Mind the Natural Way: Nutritional Solutions to Psychological Problems;* and Syd Baumel, *Dealing with Depression Naturally*

Ask your doctor about tests to see if you have toxic metals in your body.

If you have mercury amalgam fillings in your teeth, ask your dentist about tests to determine if you are sensitive to mercury and what other materials might be more compatible.

If your dentist recommends removing the fillings, get a detailed description ahead of time and ask how you will be protected from further mercury exposure while the procedure is taking place.

If you have toxic metals elsewhere in your body, ask your doctor for recommendations on how to get rid of them, including procedures for detoxification, which may include chelation therapy, a special diet or supplements.

Finally, reduce your exposure to heavy metals by avoiding aluminum pots and pans and switching to bottled or other purified water from which the heavy metals have been removed.

Chapter 11: Rule Out Blood Sugar Imbalances

"It is of great relief to the patient who feels he is going mad, or states that he is unable to cope any more, to be told that there is not a nervous breakdown round the corner, nor is his personality breaking up owing to some hidden subconscious mental conflict. What is happening is probably due to an imbalance in his metabolism involving an insufficient supply of fuel to the nervous system (i.e., low blood sugar) which in the majority of cases is easy to treat and often completely reversible."
Martin L. Budd

Few people recognize how much your blood sugar affects your mood.

Your brain can detect minute changes of as little as 2 milligrams per deciliter in your glucose level.

Even if you are doing everything else right and even if you

are not diabetic, if you are suffering from unstable blood sugar you will continue to suffer from mood swings until you change the way you eat.

I can recall working with a young woman who would check herself into the emergency room once a week from severe panic attacks even though she was taking psychiatric medication.

She started eating every 2 to 3 hours and discovered she could control the way she felt by the way she ate.

SYMPTOMS OF HYPOGLYCEMIA

Physical Symptoms
Headaches
Heart palpitations
Muscular aches and twitches
Excessive sweating
Trembling
Fainting
Double or blurred vision
Cold hands and feet

Craving for food, especially sweets
Tingling of the skin

Mental Symptoms
Depression
Fatigue
Dizziness
Confusion
Forgetfulness
Irritability
Paranoia
Anxiety
Light-headedness
Insomnia

Source: Carl C. Pfeiffer, *Mental and Elemental Nutrients: A Physician's Guide to Nutrition and Health Care*

The good news is that hypoglycemia can be corrected by improving your eating habits:

1. Eat small amounts of food every two to three hours
2. Consume protein every time you eat
3. Don't skip meals

Chapter 12: Celebrate!

"One day, in retrospect, the years of struggle will strike you as the most beautiful."
Sigmund Freud

By now, if you have worked through even 10 percent of what we have talked about, you are probably feeling better.

Whenever things are going well, determine:

1. What worked
2. What didn't work

Make a note of practitioners who are particularly helpful, flashes of insight that have come to you and any newfound understanding or appreciation for how your mind and body work together.

You may feel so much better at this point that you may be ready to give yourself permission to take a break.

Remember, the healing process has no finish line.

Relax, you are beginning to feel better!

Chapter 13: Assess Your Digestion

"It is my conviction that diagnoses such as 'schizophrenic,' 'manic depressive' and other psychotic, neurotic, or psychosomatic labels are relatively meaningless and tend only to aggravate the illness. It is the underlying organic cause that is important. We should be diagnosing paranoia caused by wheat allergy, dissociation as a manifestation of sensitivity to eggs, catatonia as a manifestation of mold or hydrocarbon allergy, and so forth, according to people's specific reactions to individual foods, chemicals, and inhalants."

William H. Philpott and Dwight K. Kalita

The cause of your depression may reside not so much in your head as in your gastrointestinal tract, including:

Difficulty absorbing vitamins and minerals from foods
Food allergies or sensitivities
Yeast overgrowth
Leaky gut syndrome, which often results from yeast overgrowth and leads to food sensitivities

Difficulty absorbing and utilizing amino acids from
  proteins
Difficulty metabolizing carbohydrates
Inadequate levels of good bacteria

Many people are surprised to learn that your gastrointestinal system is critical for your mood.

Your GI system makes about 90 percent of your serotonin, the neurotransmitter that makes you feel happy. It also makes about 300 percent more melatonin (the hormone you need to sleep deeply) than your brain. Nearly every substance that helps run and control the brain has turned up in the gastrointestinal tract.

Major neurotransmitters such as serotonin, dopamine, glutamate, norepinephrine and nitric oxide are there, too. In fact, when researchers bothered to count, they found that the gut contains 100 million neurons, way more than the spinal cord has.

Ask your health care provider about tests that examine for:

Parasites

Infections, including bacteria, yeasts and fungi

Malabsorption

Digestion efficiency, including tests for the digestion
   of carbohydrates and fats

Celiac disease

Your levels of probiotics

Chapter 14: Eliminate Yeast Infections

"Depression and manic depression, like Chronic Fatigue Syndrome, MS and other disorders can develop from many different causes. These include genetic factors, nutritional deficiencies, endocrine disturbances, viral infections, chemical sensitivities and toxicities and psychologic stress or trauma. I do not want you (or anyone) to think I'm saying that Candida albicans is the cause of depression. Yet, if you suffer from depression and/or any other disabling disorder and have a history of repeated or prolonged courses of antibiotic drugs, persistent digestive symptoms and/or recurrent vaginal yeast infections - a comprehensive treatment program which features oral antifungal medications and a special diet may enable you to change your life."

William G. Crook

The yeast called *Candida albicans* inhabits the mouth and gastrointestinal tracts of 30-50 percent of normal individuals.

In balance, yeast is among the millions of micro-organisms living alongside the healthy bacteria in the intestines that synthesize vitamins and assist the immune system.

Problems begin to occur when antibiotics, steroids, oral contraceptives and high sugar diets upset the equilibrium of normal gut flora, killing off the healthy microbes and paving the way for an overgrowth of *Candida*.

When this happens, the byproducts of *Candida* travel to the four corners of the body and begin to create many unpleasant symptoms.

If you have taken antibiotics, steroids, birth control pills or eat a lot of sugar or high fructose corn syrup, you can ask your health care professional to perform a lab test of your digestive system to determine if an imbalance is causing your depression.

As your gastrointestinal system produces more than 90

percent of your serotonin, your feel-happy neuro-transmitter, and 300 percent more of your melatonin than your brain, checking this out may be a crucial step for your healing.

SYMPTOMS LINKED TO YEAST OVERGROWTH

Depression
Hyperactivity
Anxiety
PMS
Irregular periods, painful menstruation
Intestinal problems, including gas, irritable bowel
  syndrome, colitis, diarrhea, constipation and nausea
Arthritis
Heart irregularities, including rapid heartbeat, irregular
  pulse, low or high blood pressure and chest pains
Thyroid disorders, endocrine imbalances
Vaginal yeast infections, infertility
Loss of sex drive
Food allergies and food addictions
Fatigue, dizziness, confusion, blurred vision and poor
  memory
Alcoholism

Fungal infections

Low blood sugar

Increased sensitivity to chemicals

Asthma, bronchitis, earaches, sinusitis and sore throats

Headaches

Muscle aches and weakness

Acne, hives and rashes

Immune deficiency, autoimmune diseases

Bladder and kidney problems

Sources: John Parks Trowbridge and Morton Walker, *The Yeast Syndrome: How to Help Your Doctor Identify & Treat the Real Cause of Your Yeast-Related Illness;* and William G. Crook, *The Yeast Connection*

Chapter 15: Investigate Food Reactions

"No one is suggesting that the mental hospitals are full of food-sensitive individuals who simply need an elimination diet to set them free from their illnesses. Less serious forms of mental illness, such as depression and anxiety, are commonly reported among those with food intolerance, usually accompanied by some physical symptoms. In many cases, it was the physical symptoms alone that were the target of the treatment, and both physician and patient were pleasantly surprised at the change in mood that occurred simultaneously."
Jonathan Brostoff and Linda Gamlin

The incidence of food allergy in the overall population is less than about one percent. Researchers have established, however, that a wide range of reactions falls under the general classification of food sensitivity.

A food allergy may cause a wide range of symptoms in multiple organ systems in your body and may be severe to life-threatening.

Food intolerance symptoms may be less severe but enough to adversely affect your mood.

SYMPTOMS OF FOOD SENSITIVITY

Headaches, including migraines
Fatigue, memory loss, anxiety, and hyperactivity
Depression and schizophrenia
Recurrent mouth ulcers
Muscle and joint aches, rheumatoid arthritis
Vomiting, nausea, stomach ulcers, duodenal ulcers
Diarrhea, irritable bowel syndrome, constipation, gas,
  bloating, Crohn's disease
Water retention, kidney problems
Constant runny or congested nose, asthma
Irregular heartbeat, inflammation of the capillaries
Itchy eyes, eczema, rashes, hives

Source: Jonathan Brostoff and Linda Gamlin, *Food Allergies and Food Intolerance: The Complete Guide to Their Identification and Treatment*

If you suspect you may have food sensitivities, here are several ways to identify and confirm them:

1. Blood tests conducted by your doctor

2. Applied kinesiology. A trained health care practitioner can use muscle checking to demonstrate how key organs -- especially your spleen, liver, heart and stomach -- are affected either positively or adversely by individual food constituents.

3. An elimination diet you can follow yourself. In short, you eliminate the suspected offending food from your diet for at least one week and determine if you feel better.

FOODS TO AVOID IF YOU SUSPECT YOU'RE SENSITIVE TO WHEAT OR GLUTEN GRAINS:

Barley

Rye

Oatmeal

Spelt

Breads

Bagels

Crackers

Cereal

Pretzels

Whiskey

Breaded fish and vegetables

Gravies

Hotdogs

Cookies

Candy

Pasta

Cereals

Ice cream

Pudding

Meatloaf

Processed cheese

MSG

Bouillon cubes

FOODS TO AVOID IF YOU SUSPECT YOU'RE SENSITIVE TO COW'S MILK:

Casein

Soup

Whey

Cheese

Yogurt

Breads

Butter

Coffee whitener

Bread

Sausages

Cakes

Vinegar

Puddings

Cream

Ice cream

Chocolate

Mashed potatoes

Cocoa

Sherbet

Whipped toppings

Salad dressing

Cookies

Margarine

Custard

Donuts

Cold cuts

Scrambled eggs

FOODS TO AVOID IF YOU SUSPECT YOU'RE SENSITIVE TO CORN:

Popcorn
Cereal
Corn oil
Margarine
Processed foods
Bologna
Sausage
Cornstarch
Modified food starch
Dextrin
Corn syrup
Maltodextrins
Dextrose
Lactic acid
Inositol
Sorbitol
Mannitol
Caramel color
Alcohol
Food in waxed paper cartons
Carbonated beverages
Sweetened fruit juices

Instant tea or coffee

Canned or frozen fruits

Cold cuts

Ham

Hotdogs

Jams and jellies

Canned vegetables

Catsup

Peanut butter

Chewing gum

MSG

Distilled vinegar

Many vitamins and medications

Grits

Colas

Gummed labels

Gelatin desserts

Gin

Ginger ale

Graham crackers

Whiskies, Scotch, bourbon, brandy, wine

FOODS TO AVOID IF YOU SUSPECT YOU'RE SENSITIVE TO EGGS:

Bread
Cookies
Cakes
Ice cream
Sherbet
Donuts
Beer
Pasta
Eggnog
Bouillon
Pretzels
Noodle soup
Waffles
Mayonnaise
Meringues
Root beer

Sources: Frederick Speer, *Food Allergy;* Doris J. Rapp, *Is This Your Child? Discovering and Treating Unrecognized Allergies*

BOOK III

The Stress Connection

Chapter 1: Check Your Cortisol Level

"Disease states in which alterations of the cortisol rhythm have been observed include severe depression."
Kenneth L. Becker

Cortisol is a hormone secreted by your body in response to stress.

Ask your doctor or naturopath for a saliva test to determine your current cortisol rhythm.

When we are healthy, our cortisol level is highest first thing in the morning and begins to drop off as the day progresses.

However, any disturbance in this natural rhythm may be affecting your mood.

If you would like to learn more about cortisol and how you can recover from adrenal burnout, read my most recent Amazon number one best-selling book, *Unlimited Energy Now* (Atlanta: Unlimited Energy Inc., 2014).

Cortisol is secreted by your adrenal glands (two tiny organs on top of your kidneys) whenever y o u r blood sugar levels drop.

The trouble is that a high-stress life aggravated by a lousy diet and erratic blood sugar levels will prolong a mild case of the blues and make chronic melancholia much worse.

Why? Cortisol has several effects on the body that in turn affect our emotions.

First, cortisol suppresses the function of insulin and raises blood sugar levels so we can respond well to a fight-or-flight situation.

In states of chronic stress, however, the adrenal glands have been so overstimulated that they may not be able to produce enough hormones to raise t h e blood sugar when necessary, and hypocortisolism, or Addison's disease, may result.

On the other hand, excessive production of cortisol may result in a physical disease called Cushing's syndrome, which is accompanied m o r e than half the time by psychiatric symptoms, including mania or depression.

Second, cortisol speeds the uptake of serotonin.

Low levels of serotonin have been associated with sadness, fatigue, eating disorders, suicidal thoughts and insomnia.

Animal studies suggest that cortisol acts like a barbiturate and depresses nerve cell activity in the brain.

Whether you have adrenal burnout and your cortisol level is too low, or you are cranking up your life and your cortisol is too high, either imbalance can have major detrimental effects on your mood.

PSYCHOLOGICAL SYMPTOMS OF ADRENAL DYSFUNCTION

Inability to concentrate

Excessive fatigue

Nervousness and irritability

Depression

Apprehension

Excessive weakness

Light-headedness

Faintness and fainting

Insomnia

Source: John W. Tintera, "Adrenal Dysfunction," *Hypoglycemia Association Bulletin 96*

Many researchers now believe that the blues are really a malfunction of the hypothalamic-pituitary-adrenal axis, basically a feedback loop between the hypothalamus and the pituitary gland in your brain and the adrenal glands.

If you have suffered from prolonged stress and feel depressed, you may want to ask your doctor about tests to see if your adrenal glands are functioning normally.

If they aren't, adrenal supplements are available to help you deal with the biochemical effects of your current stress while you make the changes necessary to return to good mental health.

Chapter 2: Give Yourself Permission to Lower Your Stress

"The best years of your life are the ones in which you decide your problems are your own. You don't blame them on your mother, the ecology or the president. You realize that you control your own destiny."
Albert Ellis

Sixty percent of patients with major depression meet the criteria for generalized anxiety disorder, and 30 to 90 percent of anxiety disorder patients have a history of major depression.

Hans Selye, a leading researcher on the human stress response, has theorized that melancholia may have been designed to get us to stop stressful activity before we exceed our personal, emotional and/or physical breaking points.

"By learning to gauge our own innate energy, potential weaknesses and strengths, we can all benefit from it,"

Selye comments.

"True, this requires a great deal of self-discipline and will power, but we must not lose sight of the fact that in the last analysis, each of us is responsible for his or her own well-being. Otherwise we will continue to be plagued by stress-induced diseases, no matter what treatments we devise."

Stress management is important for everyone, but it's an even higher priority for those with chronic blue funk and high levels of cortisol, the hormone secreted in response to stress.

In most individuals, cortisol levels can rise in response to a stressful event and then return to normal. That's not always the case, however, for those with chronic despondency. In some cases, cortisol levels may go up and stay up, leading to further misery.

Cortisol has a biological half-life of 13 hours, which means you will continue to feel the physical and emotional effects after a stressful event for up to 13 hours.

What helps you relax?

The more you tune in to what helps your mind and body chill out, the easier it will be for you to banish your blues for good.

Activities that help:

Meditation

Yoga, tai chi and qi gong

Walking in nature

Hobbies

Naps

Adequate sleep

Playtime

Hugs

Doing absolutely nothing

BOOK IV

The Nutrition Connection

Chapter 1: Feed Your Body What It Really Needs

"If someone had told me a year ago that I would give up bread and cheese, I would have replied, 'I'll die first,' and I felt as though I almost did. No food is worth that. There are many other pleasures, the best one being the joy of optimum health."

Charlene Grimmett

Many times when we show up at the table to eat, it's not our higher self or educated adult who's emotionally present, it's our inner brat.

Comfort yourself with the food your body really needs.

The 10 worst kinds of foods to put in your body if you have the blues:

1. Anything cooked, reheated or defrosted in a microwave oven

2. Processed foods

3. Sugar

4. Hydrogenated fats

5. Meat with antibiotics or steroids

6. Alcoholic beverages

7. Caffeine

8. Chemicals, preservatives and additives

9. Sodas and diet sodas

10. Gluten grains

The 10 best kinds of foods to put in your body to make yourself feel better:

1. Protein, as all your neurotransmitters (the brain chemicals that help you feel happy and calm) are made from amino acids, the building blocks of protein

2. Healthy fats, including coconut oil, olive oil, ghee and butter (use mostly monounsaturated and saturated oils, and avoid polyunsaturated oils unless they are pure and cold-pressed)

3. Fresh vegetables, which contain life force energy, vitamins, minerals and phytochemicals

4. Fresh fruits, which contain life force energy, vitamins, minerals and phytochemicals

5. Range-fed meats free of antibiotics and hormones

6. High-value carbohydrates, such as starchy vegetables,

legumes and gluten-free grains (if you're depressed, be sure to get enough carbohydrates for your brain to make serotonin -- a minimum of 150 grams per day, more if you are exercising)

7. Foods naturally high in probiotics (since your GI tract makes 90 percent of your serotonin), including yogurt, kefir, sauerkraut, miso soup, kombucha tea and fermented vegetables

8. Organic foods free of chemicals, pesticides, additives and other neurotoxins

9. Clean, filtered water, since your brain is 75 percent water

10. Homemade food, since you control the ingredients and know how the meal was prepared

Chapter 2: Stabilize Your Blood Sugar and Rethink Tobacco

"For many diseases of lifestyle the outlook is grim, but not so for hypoglycemia. All that is needed for the disease to go away is a change in lifestyle."
Carl C. Pfeiffer

You don't have to be clinically hypoglycemic to suffer the psychological effects of low blood sugar.

Everyone knows children who become cranky, exhausted, and tearful when they're hungry. Why should we expect to be immune to these symptoms when we grow up to be adults?

Predisposing Factors to Hypoglycemia

Overconsumption of starchy or sugary food

Smoking

Alcohol, tea and coffee

Too little or too much thyroid hormone

Vitamin and mineral deficiencies

Stress

Overgrowth of *Candida albicans*

Food sensitivities

Overproduction of insulin by the pancreas

Excessively slow or fast metabolism

Sources: Jonathan Brostoff and Linda Gamlin, *Food Allergies and Food Intolerance: The Complete Guide to Their Identification and Treatment;* William Duffy, *Sugar Blues;* Martha Sanbower, "Recognition and Treatment of Physical Factors in Psychotherapy Clients," *The Journal of Orthomolecular Medicine*

The average person consumes 20 percent of his or her

calories in some form of refined sugar.

Sometimes we think of the sugar in our diet as simply empty calories.

Perhaps a better way to think of it is as a drain on our nutritional resources.

That's because the body requires vitamins and minerals to metabolize sugar, and sugar provides us with little in return to nourish the mind or body.

Reducing or eliminating sugar can be of great assistance in not only getting you off the roller-coaster of blood sugar swings but also forcing you to eat more nutritious foods to support your immune system.

A word here on smoking.

Because cigarettes aren't a food, you may not be aware of how they affect your blood sugar levels. As you inhale, however, the addictive ingredient in cigarettes -- nicotine --

stimulates the adrenal glands to provoke the constant release of glucose into the blood.

In addition, smoking destroys vitamin C, which is a blues-fighting vitamin and an important factor in sugar metabolism.

According to the Hypoglycemia Association, every cigarette destroys about 50 milligrams of vitamin C, and the cadmium that coats the cigarette papers goes directly to the kidneys where it further deactivates zinc.

Zinc keeps our blood sugar stabilized, prevents cancer, boosts our immune function, prevents Alzheimer's disease and improves brain health and helps with the metabolism of our melatonin, which helps us to sleep soundly.

William H. Philpott, an expert in the way that common substances affect our moods, has observed that the most common psychological reaction to smoking is paranoia.

In some cases, smoking may lead to an allergy to tobacco that can cause a severe case of the blues.

Dr. Abram Hoffer, a leading researcher in

orthomolecular medicine, cured one patient who had been hospitalized for depression merely by taking him off tobacco.

Bottom line: If you want a more even disposition and higher energy levels, give up tobacco products and other stimulants.

The Hypoglycemia Association recommends beginning your dietary treatment by gradually giving up caffeine, sugar, alcohol, nicotine, grains, flours and any foods with molasses, fructose or corn sweeteners.

Chapter 3: Take Advantage of Natural Healing Remedies

"We have found that, if a drug can be found to do the job of medical healing, a nutrient can be found to do the same job. For example, antidepressants usually enhance the effect of serotonin and the epinephrines. We now know that if we give the amino acids, tryptophan or tyrosine, the body can synthesize these neurotransmitters, thereby achieving the same effect. Nutrients have fewer, milder side effects, and the challenge of the future is to replace or sometimes combine drugs with the natural healers called nutrients."
Carl C. Pfeiffer

There is no single magic pill – pharmaceutical or natural – that will banish your blues for good.

The reason this is the case is that you are biochemically unique.

The exact number is unknown, but experts believe there

may be 100 different chemical messengers in your brain.

What may bring one person into greater balance may make you feel awful.

I've made a list of natural healing remedies that may banish your blues.

For best results, I recommend you consult a nutritionist, naturopath or applied kinesiology practitioner to determine which supplements will work best for you.

Vitamins

Para Amino Benzoic Acid (PABA). A member of the B vitamins. May alleviate fatigue and depression.

Vitamin A. Potent signaling molecule in the brain. Modulates the development of new neurons. Improves learning and memory.

Vitamin B-1, also known as Thiamine. Maximizes cognitive ability. Helps the nervous system function properly.

Vitamin B-2, also known as Riboflavin. Helps the neurotransmitters in your brain carry messages. May help with insomnia, depression and mood swings.

Vitamin B-3, also known as Niacin. Helpful for memory enhancement. May help with schizophrenia and reduce the risk of Alzheimer's disease.

Vitamin B-5, also known as Pantothenic Acid. Helps to produce neurotransmitters. Required to process acetylocholine.

Vitamin B-6, also known as Pyridoxine. Needed to synthesize serotonin and dopamine. May ward off depression. A cofactor to synthesize GABA, the calming neurotransmitter.

Vitamin B-9, also known as Folic Acid/Folate, L-5-Methyltetrahydrolfolate. Crucial for cell division. May help relieve anxiety and depression. Rejuvenates the brain.

Vitamin B-12, also known as Methylcobalamin. Regulates mood and sleep cycles. Crucial for energy production.

Vitamin C. May improve mood and thinking abilities. Highest concentration found in the brain and neuroendocrine tissues. Required for the production of the neurotransmitter norepinephrine. May stabilize bipolar disorder.

Vitamin D-3. Improves anxiety and depression. Enhances nerve conduction.

Vitamin E. Important fat-soluble antioxidant for the brain. May slow cognitive decline and combat dementia. Enhances thinking abilities.

Vitamin H, also known as Biotin. Considered part of the complex of B vitamins. Helps glucose metabolism in the brain.

Vitamin K. May prevent Alzheimer's disease. Regulates calcium in the bones and the brain.

Minerals

Calcium. May improve sleep and depression and calm hyperactivity. Helps regulate secretion of neurotransmitters.

Chromium. Promotes balanced insulin handling in the brain. May help with depression, bipolar disorder and age-related mental decline.

Copper. A trace element essential for brain functions. Excess of copper can cause oxidative stress and brain damage. A buildup of copper in the brain may set up the body for Alzheimer's disease.

Iodine. Critical for normal brain development.

Iron. Essential for proper development of the brain cells that develop myelin as well as for several enzymes that produce neurotransmitters.

Lithium. Supports the health and function of the hippocampus. Lightens moods, reduces aggression. May control the extreme mood swings of bipolar disorder. May affect the levels of serotonin and norepinephrine.

Magnesium. May alleviate insomnia, depression, dizziness and muscle twitching. Improves attention span.

Manganese. Both nutritionally essential as well as potentially toxic to the brain. May reduce premenstrual syndrome. In high levels, may cause disorders similar to Parkinson's disease.

Potassium. Aids in transmitting electrical impulses in the brain. May improve brain fog.

Selenium. Important for antioxidant enzymes in the brain. Key to one of the body's master antioxidants, glutathione peroxidase (GPx). Essential for the production of thyroid hormones.

Vanadium. May increase norepinephrine and acetylcholine.

Zinc. Present in high levels in the brain. Modulates the brain's response to stress. May alleviate depression, ADHD, learning problems, violence and seizures. May prevent Alzheimer's disease. Regulates dopamine. May increase the density of serotonin receptors in the brain.

Herbs

Ashwaganda, also known as Withania Somnifera. An adaptogen that relieves stress, depression and anxiety. Enhances GABA and serotonin receptors in the brain. The roots of Ashwaganda contain tryptophan, the precursor to serotonin.

Ginger. Anti-inflammatory. Improves memory and cognition. Minimizes MSG neurotoxicity. May alleviate migraines.

Ginseng. Boosts energy. May improve memory and improve stress handling.

Gotu Kola, also known as Centella Asiatica. Antioxidant for the brain. May alleviate insomnia, anxiety and depression.

Gingko Biloba. Improves blood flow in the brain. May improve mood, motivation and memory.

Lemon Balm, also known as Melissa Officinalis. Antibacterial, antidepressant, antiviral and calming. May alleviate anxiety and depression.

Maca. Rich in B vitamins, C, E and zinc, balances the endocrine system and boosts energy. May protect against brain damage. An adaptogenic, improves the ability to respond to stress.

Macuna. Naturally contains L-Dopa, the metabolic precursor to dopamine.

Oatstraw, also known as Avena Sativa. May reduce insomnia. Calms anxiety and depression.

Passion Flower, also known as Passiflora Incarnata. Calms anxiety. May alleviate insomnia. Increases GABA levels in the brain.

Reishi Mushroom. Calming, promotes deeper sleep. Stimulates the production of nerve growth factor.

Rhodiola Rosea. Boosts mood and mental endurance. An adaptogen to improve stress handling. Increases serotonin, dopamine and norepinephrine.

Rosemary. Improves memory and circulation to the brain.

Saffron. May alleviate depression and benefit patients with Alzheimer's disease. Increases dopamine. May combat emotional overeating.

Schizandra. May alleviate depression, benefits acetylcholine in the brain. Improves stress handling.

Silymarin, also known as Milk Thistle. Antioxidant and anti-inflammatory. Although widely known to support the liver, silymarin reduces neurotoxicity.

St. John's Wort, also known as Hypericum Perforatum. Acts like a combination of serotonin, norepinephrine and dopamine. May alleviate anxiety and depression.

Turmeric, also known as Curcumin. Boosts regeneration of brain stem cells. Antioxidant and anti-inflammatory, may alleviate dementia, Alzheimer's and brain injury.

Valerian. Calming for the mind, may improve sleep.

Other Supplements

Alpha Lipoic Acid. Antioxidant that is both fat-soluble and water-soluble. Helps convert sugar into energy. May improve stroke recovery and protect against dementia.

Choline. Essential nutrient for the myelination of nerves and synthesis of acetylcholine. Important for nerve impulses to be transmitted through the nervous system.

DHEA. A precursor hormone. May improve learning and memory. Boosts nerve growth factor (NGF) and brain-derived neurotrophic factor (BDNF).

DMAE, also known as Dimethylaminoethanol. Elevates mood. Thought to increase the neurotransmitter acetylcholine, which improves memory, concentration and intellectual function. May improve quality of sleep.

Glycerophosphocholine (GPC). A building block for cell membrane phospholipids. Helps us think, sleep and remember.

Inositol. Supports relaxation. Maintains proper metabolism of serotonin. Helps with restful sleep. Improves depression, schizophrenia, Alzheimer's and attention deficit disorder.

Melatonin. Secreted by the pineal gland. Regulates sleep. An important antioxidant for the brain.

N-Acetyl-Cysteine. A precursor of glutathione, one of the most important substances for detoxification. May benefit bipolar disorder and schizophrenia.

Omega-3 Fatty Acids, EPA and DHA. Play a crucial role in brain function. Lower inflammation, combat depression, reduce mood swings. Improve learning and memory.

Phosphatidylserine. May reduce the risk of dementia and cognitive dysfunction in the elderly. Blunts the response to stress in high-intensity exercise.

SAMe, also known as S-Adenosyl Methionine. A prescription drug in Europe. Supports the metabolism of neurotransmitters in the brain. Alleviates depression and anxiety.

Amino Acids

Acetyl-L-Carnitine. Supports acetylcholine, improves memory. A powerful antioxidant can reduce the buildup of heavy metals in the brain.

Arginine. Reduces dementia. Important for normal brain functioning.

5-HTP. A compound produced by the amino acid tryptophan. A precursor to serotonin. May improve sleep, reduce addictive cravings and alleviate depression and migraines.

GABA, also known as gamma-Aminobutyric acid. The chief inhibitory neurotransmitter. Calms the mind.

Glutamine. The most abundant amino acid in the body. Removes toxic ammonia from the brain. Important during times of stress.

Glycine. Acts as an inhibitory neurotransmitter. May alleviate schizophrenia as well as brain damage from strokes. May improve memory.

Histidine. The most essential amino acid during stress. Anti-anxiety.

Isoleucine. An essential amino acid involved in the control mechanism for neurotransmitters.

Leucine. An essential amino acid involved in the control mechanism for neurotransmitters.

Lysine. Boosts attention and mental clarity.

Methionine. May improve memory and boost mood. Converted into SAMe in the liver.

Phenylalanin. Boosts neuroepinephrine and dopamine. May reduce pain and depression. Increases endorphins.

Serine. May be beneficial for treating depression, insomnia and anxiety.

Taurine. Calms the nervous system by facilitating the production of GABA. May delay cognitive decline.

Theanine. Triggers the release of GABA, a calming neurotransmitter.

Threonine. Used to make the calming amino acid glycine and the stimulating amino acid serine.

Tryptophan. Precursor to serotonin and melatonin in the brain. Improves mood, pain, sleep, eating disorders and anxiety.

Tyrosine. Supports the thyroid and adrenal gland, alleviates depression and anxiety.

Valine. Involved in the control mechanisms for neurotransmitters.

Some of my favorite natural healing remedies for the blues include flower essences.

Flower essences are vibrational remedies that work primarily on the mental, emotional and spiritual bodies.

To use flower essences, take two to four drops directly under your tongue five times per day, or put two to four drops in your water bottle.

To be effective, you will want to take the flower essences frequently, which is why most people do best when they put them in their water bottle.

There is a major acupuncture point under your tongue. When you take the flower essences under your tongue or by drinking water, the vibration circulates throughout your entire acupuncture system.

In addition, you can put two to four drops of flower essences in your bath water or use an atomizer to spray them all over your home and office to clear the energy and balance the emotional state of the space.

Some of my favorite flower essences for healing depression naturally include:

— **Being in Grace.** A large and vibrantly purple vandaceous orchid, the color of the blooms is central to the action of this essence. This essence is in part a cleansing of one's old emotional pain that can appear as physical distress or energetic blocks. Its healing process goes keenly into the emotional center of the brain; it also releases tension from the kidney meridian. www.healingorchids.com

Gorse. For when you feel great hopelessness, you've given up the belief that more can be done for you. Under persuasion or to please others, you may try different treatments, at the same time assuring those around you that there is so little hope of relief. www.bachflower.com

Mustard. This flower essence helps you when you feel suddenly depressed without reason. It feels like a cold dark cloud has destroyed all happiness and cheerfulness. The depression can lift just as suddenly for no reason. www.bachflower.com

- **Positive Outcome.** This essence helps you maintain undeterred optimism accompanied by remarkable stamina. With this essence the goal of any project is never out of sight, "like a pole-vaulter visualizing going over the bar before the run up to the big leap." Use this essence to experience being drawn forever forward. Discover how to remain positive and steadfast to your own rainbow's end. www.healingorchids.com

Red Suva Frangipani. The essence of this deep blood red Frangipani is made on the Australian coast near Darwin in the Northern Territory. It's unusual in that it doesn't have the sweet aromatic quality of other Frangipanis but rather a very heavy, musky odor. Its common name in the Pacific is "Bleeding Heart Frangipani." This essence addresses the great emotional intensity, difficulty and hardship that people can go through when a relationship is ending, close to ending, or going through a very "rocky" period. It also can be taken for the enormous initial pain and sadness of the loss of a loved one. www.ausflowers.com.au

Soul's Balm. There are times, both dark and otherwise, when we need soothing, gentle reassurance within, a healing that is both deep and quietly nurturing to the heart and soul. This unusual combination was formulated by Liz Jones, a gifted therapist who created the combination Coming Home. If a friend or family member is feeling low, this is a very good essence to offer to them. www.healingorchids.com

Sturt Desert Pea. The floral emblem of South Australia, Sturt Desert Pea is for deep hurts and sorrows. Three Aboriginal legends connect this flower to grief and sadness. It's one of the most powerful of all the essences. Like so many of the Bush Essences, it can help people bring about amazing changes in their lives. www.ausflowers.com.au

Sweet Chestnut. This essence is for those moments that happen to some people when the anguish is so great as to seem unbearable. When the mind or body feels as if it has tolerated the uttermost limits of its endurance. When it seems there is nothing but destruction and annihilation left to face. www.bachflower.com

Waratah. Waratah is for the person who is going through the "black night of the soul" and is in utter despair. It gives them the strength and courage to cope with their crisis and will bring their survival skills to the fore. This remedy also will enhance and amplify those skills. It is for emergencies and great challenges. This powerful remedy often needs to be used for only four or five days. The waratah essence is made with great assistance and guidance in profound metaphysical circumstances, from what is known to be the last flowering waratah of the season. www.ausflowers.com.au

— **Reverence.** This essence was created by the author Catherine Carrigan from the Paphiopedilum Haynaldianum orchid pictured on the cover of this book and donated to Living Tree Orchid Essences. According to Adrian Brito-Babapulle, founder of Therapeutic Energy Kinesiology (TEK), it opens and balances the 2nd, 4th, 6th, 7th, 9th, 12th 14th 17th and 21st chakras. There are also 2 connecting strands which go from the Dreaming point to points higher in the Cosmos. "It has an unusual name," Brito-Babapulle reports, "and my feeling is that the name may have been better as 'Revenant' because it appears to not only carry the essence of the orchid but appears to have a connection to higher energy beings one of which appears to be in the essence."

www.healingorchids.com.

Chapter 4: Drink Enough Water

"Pathology that is seen to be associated with 'social stresses' -- fear, anxiety, insecurity, persistent emotional and matrimonial problems -- and the establishment of depression are the results of water deficiency to the point that the water requirement of the brain is affected."
Fereydoon Batmanghelidj

One of the simplest ways to banish your despondency is to drink enough water.

All your neurotransmitters - the brain chemicals that make you happy, help you think and make you feel calm - work in water.

What are some of the symptoms you may experience if you are even slightly dehydrated?

Fatigue

High blood pressure

Skin disorders

Asthma and allergies

High cholesterol

Digestive disorders

Bladder or kidney problems

Constipation

Joint pain and joint stiffness

Weight gain

Headaches

Dizziness

Urine more yellow than normal

Dry mouth

Muscle tightness

Decreased strength

Anxiety and depression, as all your neurotransmitters work in water

Brain fog

Here are 10 tips to help you make sure you're getting enough water:

1. Drink half your body weight in ounces of water every day. In other words, your body weight divided by two = number of ounces of water you should drink daily.

2. Get a good quality water bottle. Although there are many kinds of water bottles, the best approach is to find one that's free of plastics, which can leach into the water.

3. Put a water bottle on your desk at work.

4. Put a glass of water beside your bed at night.

5. Get up first thing in the morning and drink water to get your digestive system moving. Warm water is best at this time.

6. Take a water bottle with you when you exercise. You need more water while you're working out as even slight dehydration decreases your strength.

7. If you don't like the taste of clean water, consider adding a squeeze of fresh lemon or lime.

8. You can add unsweetened cranberry juice, which cleanses your kidneys.

9. Consider putting a filter on your kitchen sink, as a study by the National Resources Defense Council of water in 19 U.S. cities found problems with pollution, old pipes and outdated treatment facilities.

10. Consider leasing a water dispenser for your home or office. We recently began using a dispenser for distilled water after my partner, Ken Holmes, learned

that inventor Alexander Graham Bell cured himself of rheumatoid arthritis and sciatica by drinking distilled water.

Having clean water is a privilege of living in the civilized Western world.

It's estimated that 780 million people worldwide lack access to clean water. To put it into perspective, that's 2.5 times the total population of the United States!

Make an effort to drink more water and notice how your energy and overall health improve dramatically.

BOOK V

Think Yourself Happy

Chapter 1: Rethink the Real Reason to Exercise

"Aerobic exercise is more effective than placebo and no treatment, and it is as effective as group psychotherapy, individual psychotherapy and meditation/relaxation."
Siegfried Weyerer and Brigitte Kupfer

Many people are taught that working out benefits only the physical body, only to change their mind when they experience the profound beneficial effects for your mood:

1. Physical activity relieves stress, a major contributor to the blues.

2. Endorphins released into the brain during a good workout lift the mood.

3. According to Eastern tradition, exercise cools the liver and assists in detoxifying the body of substances that might interfere with brain functioning.

4. Exercise improves self-confidence and a feeling of mastery over one's body.

5. Deep breathing during exercise can allow for a form of meditation.

6. Regular workouts reinforce the importance of nurturing yourself.

In 2000, Duke University researchers published a study showing that exercise alone was more effective for treating the blues than antidepressants alone or antidepressants and exercise combined.

"We had assumed that exercise and medication together would have had an additive effect, but this turned out not to be the case," said Duke psychologist James Blumenthal.

Only about 20 percent of the population get enough aerobic exercise at a level to benefit their cardiovascular system.

The good news is that you don't have to do only aerobic

activities that accelerate the heart rate over a long period of time to benefit psychologically.

In fact, one group of researchers found that men who practiced yoga had lower levels of tension, fatigue and anger than those who swam regularly.

One survey of the effects of the gentlest mind-body exercises - such as the Feldenkrais Method, tai chi, yoga, the Alexander Technique, Pilates, and qi gong -- found demonstrable decreases in anxiety levels and even dramatic improvements in body chemistry, such as improved glucose tolerance and reduced responsiveness to stress hormones.

Study after study has found that the most sedentary, even obese, and even wheelchair-bound individuals can benefit from some kind of regular program regardless of whether they improve their overall physical fitness.

The best explanation I've found comes from brilliant physicist Moshe Feldenkrais, who found himself in the unlikely role of inventing a whole new system of movement when he became confined to a wheelchair.

Feldenkrais observed that four components make up every waking state: sensation, feeling, thought and movement.

In other words, for every state of mind, there will be corresponding patterns of spatial and rhythmic changes in the body, including changes in breathing, eating, speaking, blood circulation and even digestion.

The brain's motor cortex, where patterns activating the muscles are established, lies only a few millimeters above the structures that process and associate emotions.

"Owing to the close proximity to the motor cortex of the brain structures dealing with thought and feeling, and the tendency of processes in the brain tissue to diffuse and spread to neighboring tissues, a drastic change in the motor cortex will have parallel effects on thinking and feeling," Feldenkrais wrote in his book *Awareness Through Movement*.

Simply put, to change how you feel, change what you are doing with your body.

If these explanations aren't convincing enough, I offer this warning: If you don't exercise, you will be at significantly higher risk for developing the blues or increasing the severity of any heavyheartedness you already have.

Men who don't exercise are more than 12 times more likely to be depressed than those who do.

A very good question to ask yourself may be how much activity you need to combat the blues.

Studies show that just 10 minutes of walking boosts brain chemistry to increase your happiness.

When you walk or perform other forms of exercise, you release brain-derived neurotrophic factor (BDNF), a substance that repairs the memory neurons in your brain, effectively acting as a reset switch.

Find the physical movement that feels most comfortable for you at this time, whether it is a daily walk, an exercise class, a run around the park or something easier.

Chapter 2: Create Your Life With Your Thoughts

"You must master a new way to think before you can master a new way to be."
Marianne Williamson

A belief is just a thought you have been thinking over and over again.

What we believe is what we tend to experience because we project our beliefs out into the world onto other people and situations.

Therefore, changing our beliefs and our thoughts is crucial for transforming our experience.

One strategy to promote positive thinking is to use affirmations. Good examples include:

I am content and all my needs are satisfied.

I relax, do my best, and the world is beautiful.

I am connected to my higher power.

I let go of the past to allow beneficial changes.

I allow only the most positive energy to enter my body, mind, and spirit.

I convert all energy that comes to me into gifts of love for myself and others.

I flow with joy.

Create your own affirmations to manifest what you want to experience in your life.

Make each affirmation positive, active and so clear that even a child can understand.

There are many ways to make affirmations part of your everyday life:

Begin each day by writing a page of positive affirmations in your journal.

Devote commuting time to work for silent prayers of thanks, as if what you have affirmed has come true already.

Take note of your prayers and how each one is answered.

Conclude every day by noticing all the ways you have been blessed.

Chapter 3: Do Unto Others

"Spread love where ever you go. Let no one ever come to you without leaving happier."
Mother Theresa

One of the simplest ways to banish your own bad mood is to create a better life for somebody else.

The fact that giving to others is a major boost to your own mood has been documented by scientific research.

The point is to get out of your own way, see beyond your own aches and pains and make a difference for other people, your community, even the planet.

Why is this so important?

One of the ways to be happy in life is through life meaning.

We receive a feel deeply rewarded through contributing to the lives of others.

Conversely, if we stay stuck on our own troubles and woes, we lose sight of the fact that other people may be suffering at even greater depth than we are.

Human life doesn't go by without a series of challenges.

Ask yourself the following questions:

1. If I could make a difference to even just one person, who would that be?

2. What are the unique gifts that I have that could be of service to others? It could be something as simple as making people laugh, cooking a meal that only you know how to prepare so well, or being present with people in a time of crisis when no one else is there to console them.

3. If I could make a contribution to others that would bring me the greatest joy, what would that be?

I often think of my garden.

Of course, it brings me joy every time I look out the window or take a walk along the paths. But I also recognize that I've created a sanctuary where other people can pause, ponder and remember that life is beautiful.

Chapter 4: Bless Your Lesson

"There is no antidepressant that will cure a depression which is spiritually based, because the malaise does not originate from brain dysfunction but from an accurate response to the desecration of life. The body is the reflection of the spirit in its physical expression, and its problems are the dramatization of the struggles of the spirit which gives it life. A belief that we ascribe to 'out there' has its effect 'in here.' Everyone dies by his own hand. That is a hard clinical fact, not a moral view."
David R. Hawkins

Victor Frankl, a psychiatrist who survived the Nazi death camps, believed that happiness lies not so much in a life of ease but in a life of purpose.

In his great work, *Man's Search For Meaning*, Frankl wrote: "Ultimately, man should not ask what the meaning of his life is, but rather that it is he who is asked.

"In a word, each man is questioned by life; and he can only answer to life by answering for his own life; to life he can only respond by being responsible."

When you are feeling hopeless and blue, the last thing you actually think is that you are being blessed. A blue period, however, can become a major life blessing.

Ask yourself these questions:

1. What in my life is no longer serving me?

2. Am I being called to break down and let go of major structures in my life that have lost their meaning in order to make room for something even better?

3. How can I make good use of this time

to dive into myself and discover what matters to me now?

When you go through these periods, life usually keeps beating you up until you get the message that it is time for you to make a change.

Making shifts to something better may not always be easy. As you emerge on the other side, however, you will inevitably discover the wisdom of letting go.

CONCLUSION

Chapter 1: Thank You

"The sun is always shining; you need only remove the clouds."
David R. Hawkins

Thank you so much for taking the time to read *Banish the Blues Now*.

It is my prayer that this book gives you greater insight into how you can feel better day by day.

So many people who are prescribed psychiatric medications get the impression that drugs are the only way to make themselves feel better.

Many people take these medications but don't end up feeling much better.

The labels and diagnoses they are given hang around their character like deep judgments, making them feel hopeless to improve and fearful of their inner nature.

I know this information works because I have been free of psychiatric medications for 22 years.

My life, like all lives, has had its ups and downs, but year by year I get stronger inside.

Perhaps there is nothing truly wrong with you.

Maybe you just need to learn how to manage yourself a little bit better.

Chapter 2: Prayer for My Reader

"The best way out is always through."
Robert Frost

I give this book to you, my dear reader, in the form of a prayer from my heart to your heart.

Heavenly Father, Dear God,
Thank you for blessing us with this information.
Please allow each of us to take these words to heart and make this wisdom our own.
Please bless each person who reads this book with light, love and hope for the future.
Please guide each reader to the information that is most important at this time in their lives.
Give us all strength and courage to embrace the lives with which we have been so blessed.
Bless us all with inner peace.
Guide us to the experience of joy and happiness.
Thank you God, thank you God. Amen.

BIBLIOGRAPHY

"An Adequate Breakfast,"*Hypoglycemia Association Bulletin* 95 (July-Aug. 1977).

Aihara, Herman. *Acid & Alkaline.* Oroville, CA: George Ohsawa Macrobiotic Foundation, 1986.

"Alcoholism," *Mastering Food Allergies* 5, no.1 (Dec.-Jan.1990).

"Americans Doing Better at Eating Their Veggies," Medical Tribune News Service, Dec. 15, 1995.

Andreani, D., P.J. Lefebvre, V. Marks and G. Tamburrano, eds. *Recent Advances in Hypoglycemia.* New York: Raven Press, 1992.

Appleton, Nancy. *Lick the Sugar Habit.* Garden City Park, NY: Avery Publishing Group, 1988.

Arky, Ronald, ed. *Physicians' Desk Reference.* Montvale, NJ: Medical Economics Co., 1997.

Asaad, Ghazi. *Understanding Mental Disorders Due to Medical Conditions or Substance Abuse.* New York: Brunner/Mazel, 1995.

Avery, Phyllis. *Stop Your Indigestion: Causes, Remedies, Recipes.* Vista, CA: Hygeia Publishing Co., 1993.

Ballantyne, Bryan, Timothy Marrs and Paul Turner, eds. *General and Applied Toxicology,* Vols. 1 and 2. New York: Stockton Press, 1993.

Ballentine, Rudolph. *Diet and Nutrition.* Honesdale, PA: Himalayan International Institute, 1978.

Bartlett, John, ed. *Familiar Quotations.* Boston: Little Brown and Co., 1882.

Batmanghelidj, F. *Your Body's Many Cries for Water.* Falls Church, VA: Global Health Solutions, 1992.

Baumel, Syd. *Dealing with Depression Naturally.* New Canaan, CT: Keats Publishing, 1995.

Becker, Kenneth L., ed., *Principles and Practice of Endocrinology and Metabolism,* 2d ed. Philadelphia: J.B. Lippincott & Co., 1995.

"A Beneficial Effect of Calcium Intake on Mood," *Journal of Orthomolecular Medicine* 9, no. 4 (fourth quarter 1994).

"Biodetoxification," *Mastering Food Allergies* 35 (1989).

Blakeslee, Sandra. "Brain in the Gut Makes Gut Reactions," *The New York Times,* Jan.23,1996.

Bland, Jeffrey S. "A Functional Approach to Mental Illness: A New Paradigm for Managing Brain Biochemical Disturbances," *Townsend Letter For Doctors,* Dec. 1994.

Bourne, Ronald F. "Serotonin: The Neurotransmitter for the '90s," *Drug Topics,* Oct. 10, 1994.

Breggins, Peter R. *Toxic Psychiatry: Why Therapy, Empathy, and Love Must Replace the Drugs, Electroshock, and Biochemical Theories of the "New Psychiatry."* New York: St. Martin's Press, 1991.

Brennan, Barbara Ann. *Hands of Light.* New York: Bantam Books, 1988.

Breneman, James C. *Basics of Food Allergy.* Springfield, IL: Charles C. Thomas Publisher, 1984.

Bricklin, Mark. *Prevention Magazine's Nutrition Advisor.* Emmaus, PA: Rodale Press, 1993.

Brostoff, Jonathan, and Linda Garnlin. *The Complete Guide to Food Allergy and Intolerance.* New York: Crown Publishers, 1989.

Brostoff, Jonathan, and Stephen J, Challacombe. *Food Allergy and Intolerance.* London: Bail-Here Tindall, 1987.

Budd, Martin L. *Low Blood Sugar (Hypoglycemia): The 20th-Century Epidemic?* New York: Sterling Publishing Co., 1983.

Buffaloe, Adrienne. "Chemical Sensitivity: It's a More Serious Problem More Often Than You Think," http://accessnewage.com/articles/health/chemical.htm

Calbom, Cherie, and Maureen Keane. *Juicing for Life.* Garden City Park, NY: Avery Publishing Group, 1992.

Carper, Jean. *Food - Your Miracle Medicine.* New York: HarperCollins, 1993.

Casdorph, H. Richard, and Morton Walker. *Toxic Metal Syndrome: How Metal Poisonings Can Affect Your Brain.* Garden City Park, NY: Avery Publishing, 1995.

"Cerebral Allergies," *Mastering Food Allergies* 3, no. 5 (May 1988).

Chaitow, Leon. *Thorsons Guide to Amino Acids.* London: Thorsons, 1991.

Childre, Doc Lew. *Freeze-Frame: Fast Action Stress Relief: A Scientifically Proven Technique.* Boulder Creek, CA: Planetary Publications, 1995.
Clinical Chemistry, 40, no. 2 (1994), pp. 296-302.

"Clinging To Their Bottles," *Taste Matters, American Council on Exercise* 3, no. 1 (Jan.-Feb. 1997).

Conning, D.M., and A.B.G. Lansdown. *Toxic Hazards in Food.* New York: Raven Press, 1983.

Cope, Cuthbert L. *Adrenal Steroids and Disease,* 2d ed. Philadelphia: J.B. Lippincott Co., 1972.

Cotton, Richard T., ed. *Aerobics Instructor Manual.* San Diego, CA: American Council on Exercise, 1993.

"Critical Issues in the Treatment of Affective Disorders." *Depression* 3 (1995).

Crook, William G. *The Yeast Connection.* Jackson, TN: Professional Books, 1984.

Crook, William G. *The Yeast Connection and the Woman.* Jackson, TN: Professional Books, 1995.

"CSF 5-HIAA Predicts Suicide Risk After Attempted Suicide," *Suicide & Life-Threatening Behavior,* 24, no. 1 (1994).

David, T.J. *Food and Food Additive Intolerance in Childhood.* London: Blackwell Scientific Publications, 1993.

Dennestein, Lorraine, and Ian Fraser, eds. *Hormones and Behavior.* New York: Excerpta Medica, 1986.

Depue, Richard A. *Psychobiology of the Depressive Disorders: Implications for the Effects of Stress.* New York: Academic Press, 1979.

"Detoxification," *Nutritional Pearls* 24. Marietta, GA: Metagenics (n.d.).

"The Detoxification Supplementation Therapy: A Shortcut to the Recovery of the Mental and Degenerative Diseases," *The Journal of Orthomolecular Medicine* 9, no. 4 (fourth quarter, 1980).

Dickey, Thomas, ed. *The Wellness Encyclopedia of Food and Nutrition.* New York: Health Letter Associates, 1992.

Duffy, William. *Sugar Blues.* New York: Warner Books, 1975.

Eliot, T.S. *The Four Quartets.* London: Faber and Faber, 1976.

"Emotions Impact on Allergies," *Mastering Food Allergies* 9, no. 4 (July-Aug. 1994).

Erasmus, Udo. *Fats That Heal Fats That Kill.* Burnaby, B.C.: Alive Books, 1993.

Erdman, Robert. *The Amino Revolution.* New York: Simon and Schuster, 1987.

Extein, Irl, and Mark S. Gold, eds. *Medical Mimics of Psychiatric Disorders.* Washington, D.C.: American Psychiatric Press, 1986.

Feldenkrais, Moshe. *Awareness Through Movement.* New York: Harper & Row, 1977.

Fox, Arnold, and Barry Fox. *DLPA to End Chronic Pain and Depression.* New York: Pocket Books, 1985.

Frankl, Viktor E. *Man's Search for Meaning.* New York: Touchstone Books, 1984.

Frazier, Claude A. *Coping with Food Allergy.* New York: New York Times Book Co., 1974.

Fredericks, Carlton. *Carlton Fredericks' New Low Blood Sugar and You.* New York: Putnam Publishing, 1985.

Friend, Kathleen D., and Carol L. Alter. "T4 Therapy in Depression and Hypothyroidism," *Depression* 2 (1994/1995).

Gerber, Richard. *Vibrational Medicine: New Choices for Healing Ourselves.* Sante Fe, NM: Bear & Co., 1988.

Glassburn, Vicki. *Who Killed Candida?* Brushton, NY: TEACH Services Inc., 1991.

Golos, Natalie, and Frances Golos Golbitz. *If This Is Tuesday, It Must Be Chicken.* New Canaan, CT: Keats Publishing, 1983.

Grimmett, Charlene. *Beat the Yeast Cookbook.* Aurora, IL: Charlene Grimmett, 1985.

Hannaford, Carla. *Smart Moves: Why Learning Is Not All In Your Head.* Arlington, VA: Great Ocean Publishers, 1995.

Hathcock, John N. *Nutritional Toxicology, Vol. I.* New York: Academic Press, 1982.

Hawkins, David R. *Power vs. Force: An Anatomy of Consciousness.* Sedona, AZ: Veritas Publishing, 1995.

Health Response Ability Systems, Inc., "Preventing Food-Borne Illness," HRS Health Knowledge Center, AOL Health and Medical Forum (America Online), 1995.

"Health Risks of the 21 Most Common Chemicals Found in 31 Fragrance Products by a 1991 E.P.A. Study," http://www.ourlittleplace.com/chemicals.html

Himwich, Harold Edwin. *Biochemistry, Schizophrenia and Affective Illnesses.* Baltimore: Williams and Wilkins, 1971.

Hofeldt, Fred D. *Preventing Reactive Hypoglycemia: The Great Medical Dilemma.* St. Louis: Warren H. Green, Inc., 1983.

Hoes, M.J.A.J.M. "Stress and Strain: Their Definition, Psychobiology, and Relationship to Psychosomatic Medicine." *The Journal of Orthomolecular Medicine* 1, no. 1 (first quarter 1986).

"How Much Does Depression Cost Society?" *Harvard Mental Health Letter,* Oct. 1994.

"How Pure Is your Water?" *Delicious* 11, no. 4 (April 1995). Huggins, Hal A. *It's All in Your Head.* Garden City Park, NY: Avery Publishing Group, 1993.

Hunter, J.O. "Food Allergy or Enterometabolic Disorder?" *Lancet 338* (Aug. 1991).

"Hypoglycemia, The Modern Holistic Approach: A Talk by Mark S. Smith," *Hypoglycemia Association Bulletin* 185 (n.d.).

"Hypothyroidism: A Missed Diagnosis." *The Felix Letter: A Commentary on Nutrition* 42 (1988).

"Investigations of the Cellular Immunity During Depression and the Free Interval: Evidence for an Immune Activation in Affective Psychosis," *Progress in Neuro-Psychopharmacology and Biological Psychiatry* 17 (1993).

Jacobson, Michael F. *Eater's Digest: The Consumer's Factbook of Food Additives.* Garden City, NY: Doubleday & Co., 1972.

Jacobson, Michael F., Lisa Y. Lefferts, and Anne Witte Garland. *Safe Food: Eating Wisely in a Risky World.* New York: Berkeley Books, 1993.

Jones, Marjorie Hurt. *The Allergy Self-Help Cookbook.* Emmaus, PA: Rodale Press, 1984.

Justice, Blair. *Who Gets Sick?* New York: Tarcher, 1988. Kanarek, Robin B., and Robin Marks-Kaufman. *Nutrition and Behavior: New Perspectives.* New York: Van Nostrand Reinhold, 1991.

Koranyi, Erwin K., ed. *Physical Illness in the Psychiatric Patient.* Springfield, IL: Charles C. Thomas Publisher, 1982.

Kunin, Richard A. *Meganutrition.* New York: New American Library, 1981.

La Forge, Ralph. *Mind-Body Fitness: Encouraging Prospects for Primary and Secondary Prevention Programs.* San Diego, CA: San Diego Cardiac Center Medical Group, 1996.

Lazarus, Pat. *Healing the Mind the Natural Way: Nutritional Solutions to Psychological Problems.* New York: G.P. Putnam's Sons, 1995.

Lappe, Frances Moore. *Diet for a Small Planet.* New York: Ballantine Books, 1982.

Lawson, Lynn. *Staying Well in a Toxic World.* Chicago: Noble Press, 1993.

"Leaky Gut: A Common Problem with Food Allergies," *Mastering Food Allergies* 7, no. 5 (Sept.-Oct. 1993).

"Lithium-Thyroid Interactive Hypothesis of Neuropsychological Deficits: A Review and Proposal" *Depression* 1 (1994/1995).

MacMahon, Brian, and Takashi Sugimura. *Coffee and Health (Banbury Report).* Cold Spring Harbor, NY: Cold Spring Harbor Laboratory, 1984.

"Magnesium and Health," *Vitamin Research Products Nutritional News,* July 1993.

Mandell, Marshall, and Lynne Waller Scanlon. *Dr. Mandell's 5-Day Allergy Relief System.* New York: Pocket Books, 1979.

Matheny, Kenneth B., and Richard J. Riordan. *Stress and Strategies for Lifestyle Management.* Atlanta: Georgia State University Business Press, 1992.

Miller, Klara. *Toxicological Aspects of Food.* London: Elsevier Applied Science, 1987.

Minirth, Frank B., and Paul D. Meier. *Happiness Is a Choice.* Grand Rapids, MI: Baker Book House, 1988.

"Mood Alteration with Yoga and Swimming: Aerobic Exercise May Not Be Necessary," *Perceptual Motor Skills* 75 (1992).

Nerozzi, Dina, Frederick K. Goodwin, and Erminio Costa, eds. *Hypothalamic Dysfunction in Neuropsychiatric Disorders.* New York: Raven Press, 1987.

Newbold, H.L. *Mega-Nutrients for Your Nerves.* New York: Berkeley Books, 1981.

Newbold, H.L. *Dr.Newbold's Nutrition for Your Nerves.* New Canaan, CT: Keats Publishing, 1993.

"Nicotine Addiction and Schizophrenia," *The Journal of Orthomolecular Medicine* 5, no. 3 (1990).

Null, Gary. *No More Allergies.* New York: Villard Books, 1992.

Nutrition and the Mind. New York: Four Walls Eight Windows, 1995.

Odds, F.C. *Candida and Candidosis.* Baltimore: University Park Press, 1979.

"One Reason You May Fail To Get Well -- Even On Best Diet," *Mastering Food Allergies* 42 (1990).

Palgrave, Francis T. *The Golden Treasury.* New York: MacMillan Co., 1956.

Pauling, Linus. *How to Live Longer and Feel Better.* New York: Avon Books, 1987.

Pfeiffer, Carl C. *Nutrition and Mental Illness.* Rochester, VT: Healing Arts Press, 1987.

Pfeiffer, Carl C., *Mental and Elemental Nutrients.* New Canaan, CT: Keats Publishing, 1975.

Philpott, William H., and Dwight G. Kalita. *Brain Allergies: The Psychonutrient Connection.* New Canaan, CT: Keats Publishing, 1980.

Pierrakos, John C. *Core Energetics.* Mendocino, CA: Life Rhythm, 1990.

"Plasma Concentrations of Gamma-Aminobutyric Acid (GABA) and Mood Disorders: A Blood Test for Manic Depressive Disease?" *Clinical Chemistry* 40, no. 2 (1994).

"Plasma Ratios of Tryptophan and Tyrosine to Other Large Neutral Amino Acids in Manic Depressive Patients," *Journal of Psychiatry & Neurology* 46, no. 3 (1992).

"Plasma Tryptophan Levels and Plasma Tryptophan/Neutral Amino Acids Ratio in Patients with Mood Disorder, Patients with Obsessive-Compulsive Disorder, and Normal Subjects," *Psychiatry Research* 44, no. 2 (1992).

Price, Lawrence H., and George R. Heninger, "Lithium in the Treatment of Mood Disorders," *The New England Journal of Medicine,* Sept. 1, 1994.

Randolph, Theron G., and Ralph W. Moss. *An Alternative Approach to Allergies,* rev. ed. New York: Harper & Row, 1989.

Rapp, Doris J., *Is This Your Child Discovering and Treating Unrecognized Allergies in Children and Adults.* New York: William Morrow and Co., 1991.

Rea, William J, *Chemical Sensitivity: Principles and Mechanisms.* Boca Raton, FL: Lewis Publishers, 1992.

"Relationship Between Irritable Bowel Syndrome and Double Depression," *Depression* 3 (1996).

Richardson, Malcolm D., and David W. Warnock. *Fungal Infection: Diagnosis and Management.* Boston: Blackwell Scientific Publications, 1993.

"The Risks of Excessive Drinking," The Coalition for Consumer Health and Safety Web Site: Hidden Hazards, http://www.essential.org./ cchs.hh.html#Alcohol.

Robinson, Robert G., and Peter V. Rabins. *Aging and Clinical Practice: Depression and Coexisting Disease.* New York: Igaku-Shoin, 1989.

Rochlitz, Steven. *Allergies and Candida: With the Physicist's Rapid Solution.* New York: Human Ecology Balancing Sciences, 1989.

Rogers, Sherry. *The E. I. Syndrome.* Syracuse, NY: Prestige Publishers, 1986.

You Are What You Ate: An Rx for the Resistant Diseases of the 21st Century. Syracuse, NY: Prestige Publishing, 1988.

Rosenthal, M. Sara. *The Thyroid Sourcebook.* Los Angeles: Lowell House, 1995.

Rosenvold, Lloyd. *Can A Gluten-Free Diet Help?* New Canaan, CT: Keats Publishing, 1992.

Ross, Harvey M. *Fighting Depression.* New Canaan, CT: Keats Publishing, 1992.

Roth, June. *The food/depression connection.* Chicago: Contemporary Books, Inc., 1978.

"The Rotary Diversified Diet," *Mastering Food Allergies* 1, no. 6 (June 1986).

Salaman, Maureen. *Foods That Heal.* Menlo Park, CA: Stratford Publishing, 1989.

Sanbower, Martha. "Recognition and Treatment of Physical Factors in Psychotherapy Clients," *Journal of Orthomolecular Medicine* 5, no. 2.

"Manic Depression: An Alternate Treatment," *Journal of Orthomolecular Medicine* 2, no. 3.

"Schizophrenia and Bipolar Disorder May Be On a Continuum," The Schizophrenia-Bipolar Interface: Current Research and Future Directions. Presented at the 1995 International Stanley Foundation Satellite Symposium, organized by Dr. E. Fuller Torrey. Stanley Foundation Web Site, www/nami.org/about/stanley.htm.

Schulkin, Jay, ed. *Hormonally Induced Changes in Mind and Body.* New York: Academic Press, 1993.

Schultz, Dorothy. "The Information Super Highway," *Hypoglycemia Association Bulletin* 197 (Oct.-Dec. 1995).

Schwartz, George R. *In Bad Taste: The MSG Syndrome.* Santa Fe, NM: Health Press, 1988.

Seligman, Martin E.P. *Learned Optimism.* New York: Alfred A. Knopf, 1991.

Service, F. John. *Hypoglycemic Disorders.* Boston: G.K. Hall Medical Publishers, 1983.

"Seventy-Two Percent of Americans Are Magnesium-Deficient," *Better Nutrition for Today's Living* 57 (March 1995).

Shinn, Florence Scovel. *The Wisdom of Florence Scovel Shinn.* New York: Fireside, 1989.

Siegel, George J., Bernard W. Agranoff, R. Wayne Albers, and Perry B. Molinoff, eds. *Basic Neurochemistry: Molecular, Cellular, and Medical Aspects*, 4th ed. New York: Raven Press, 1989.

"Significantly Increased Expression of T-Cell Activation Markers in Depression: Further Evidence for an

Inflammatory Process During That Illness," *Progress in Neuro-Psychopharmacology and Biological Psychiatry* 17 Slagle, Priscilla. *The Way Up From Down.* New York: St. Martin's Paperbacks, 1992.

Smart Basics Inc. "Smart Basics Glossary: Amino Acids," 1996, http://www/vrcreations.com/index.html.

"Smart Basics Minerals Glossary," 1996, http://www.smartbasic.com/glos.minerals.dir.html.

Smith, Marge. "Feeding Yourself in All Sorts of Circumstances," *Hypoglycemia Association Bulletin* 164 (Sept. 1995).

Smolinske, Susan C. *CRC Handbook of Food, Drug, and Cosmetic Excipients.* Boca Raton, FL: CRC Press, 1992.

Speer, Frederick. *Food Allergy.* Boston: PSG Inc., 1983.

Stegink, Lewis D., and L.J. Filer Jr., eds. *Aspartame.* New York: Marcel Dekker Inc., 1984.

"Steroid Hormones, Clinical Correlates," Diagnos-Techs Inc. Seminar in Atlanta, GA, October 1995.

Sudy, Mitchell, ed. *Personal Trainer Manual.* San Diego, CA: American Council on Exercise, 1991.

Thie, John. *Touch For Health: A New Approach to Restoring Our Natural Energy.* Sherman Oaks, CA: T.H. Enterprises, 1994.

"The Treatment of Depression: Prescribing Practices of Primary Care Physicians and Psychiatrists," *The Journal of Family Practice* 35, no. 6 (1992).

Tintera, John W. "Adrenal Dysfunction," *Hypoglycemia Association Bulletin* 96 (n.d.).

Trowbridge, John Parks, and Morton Walker. *The Yeast Syndrome.* New York: Bantam Books, 1986.

Tunbridge, W.M.G. *Thyroid Disease: The Facts.* Oxford: Oxford University Press, 1991.

"Update on Mood Disorders," *The Harvard Mental Health Letter,* Dec. 1994.

"U.S. Tap Water Is Dirty," Associated Press Report, June 1, 1995.

Weyerer, Siegfried, and Brigitte Kupfer. "Physical Exercise and Psychological Health!" *Sports Medicine* 17, no. 2.

Whybrow, Peter C. "Sex Differences in Thyroid Axis Function: Relevance to Affective Disorder and Its Treatment," *Depression* 3 (1995).

Wilson, Cynthia. *Chemical Exposure and Human Health.* Jefferson, NC: McFarland and Co., 1993:

Wolstenholme, G.E.W., and Ruth Porter. *The Human Adrenal Cortex: Its Function Throughout Life.* Boston: Little, Brown and Co., 1967.

Wurtman, Richard J., and Judith J. Wurtman. "Carbohydrates and Depression," *Scientific American,* Jan. 1989.

Nutrition and the Brain, Vol. 4. New York: Raven Press, 1979.

"X-Linked Dominant Manic-Depressive Illness," *The Journal of Orthomolecular Psychiatry* 8, no. 2.

Zamm, Alfred V. "Removal of Dental Mercury: Often an Effective Treatment for the Very Sensitive Patient," *The Journal of Orthomolecular Medicine* 5, no. 3 (third quarter 1990).

Ziff, Sam, and Michael F. Ziff. *Dentistry Without Mercury.* Orlando, FL: Bio-Probe Inc., 1993.

About The Author

I have the ability to get to the heart of the matter and figure out what will actually work to make you radiantly healthy.

Hi, my name is Catherine Carrigan.

I am a medical intuitive healer.

The average person who comes to see me has seen at least seven other practitioners -- medical doctors, psychologists, psychiatrists, chiropractors, shamans, homeopaths, physiotherapists, nutritionists, herbalists, acupuncturists -- you name it.

I offer a comprehensive system that begins with figuring out what is actually going on with you and then putting together a personalized plan that empowers you to achieve levels of health you may not have even thought possible.

I don't need to see you or put my hands on you to know what is wrong or what will make you better.

I have a passion for healing, and I can teach you how to become healthy using natural methods, including the very best mix of therapeutic exercise, nutrition and energy medicine.

You can connect with me on Facebook at: https://www.facebook.com/catherinecarriganauthor

Follow me on Twitter at https://twitter.com/CSCarrigan

Read my blog at www.catherinecarrigan.com

Follow my website at www.unlimitedenergynow.com

Connect with me on LinkedIn at: www.linkedin.com/in/catherinecarrigan/

Sign up for my newsletter at: http://bit.ly/1C4CFOC

You can read testimonials from my clients here:

http://catherinecarrigan.com/testimonials/

http://unlimitedenergynow.com/testimonials/

Training in Fitness

- Certified Personal Fitness Trainer: A.C.E. certified in Personal Fitness Training
- Corrective High-Performance Exercise Kinesiologist (C.H.E.K) Practitioner, Level I: C.H.E.K. Institute.
- Certified Group Exercise Instructor: A.C.E. certified in Group Exercise
- A.C.E. Specialty Recognitions: Strength training and Mind-Body Fitness
- Exercise Coach, C.H.E.K. Institute
- Certified Yoga Teacher: 500-hour Yoga Teacher through Lighten Up Yoga; six 200-hour certifications through Integrative Yoga Therapy, the White Lotus Foundation, and the Atlanta Yoga Fellowship, Lighten Up Yoga and Erich Schiffmann teacher training (twice)
- Practitioner of qi gong, Chinese martial arts
- Certified Older Adult Fitness Trainer through the American Institute of Fitness Educators

Training in Nutrition

- Food Healing Level II Facilitator

- Holistic Lifestyle Coach though the C.H.E.K. Institute, Level 3

- Certified Sports Nutritionist through the American Aerobics Association International/International Sports Medicine Association

- Author, *Healing Depression: A Holistic Guide* (New York: Marlowe and Co., 1999), a book discussing nutrition and lifestyle to heal depression without drugs

- Schwarzbein Practitioner though Dr. Diana Schwarzbein, an expert in balancing hormones naturally

Training in Healing

- Specialized Kinesiology through Sue Maes of London, Ontario, Canada

- Self-Empowerment Technology Practitioner

- Brain Gym, Vision Circles and Brain Organization instructor through the Educational Kinesiology Foundation

- Touch for Health

- Thai Yoga Body Therapy

- Flower Essence Practitioner

- Reiki Master, Usui tradition

- Life Coaching through Sue Maes' Mastering Your Knowledge Mentorship Program and Peak Potentials

- Medical Intuitive Readings and Quantum Healing

Other Training

- Health and fitness columnist

- Playwright of 12 plays, three produced in New York City

- Past Spokesperson, the Depression Wellness Network

- Phi Beta Kappa graduate of Brown University

- Former national spokesperson for Johnson & Johnson

- Owner and co-host, Total Fitness Radio Show

About the Cover

"You are not here to verify,
Instruct yourself, or inform curiosity
Or carry report. You are here to kneel
Where prayer has been valid. And prayer is more
Than an order of words, the conscious occupation
Of the praying mind, or the sound of the voice praying."
T.S. Eliot, "Little Gidding" of The Four Quartets

This Paphiopedilum Haynaldianum orchid began blooming in my studio in April 2015 while I was arriving at the culmination of this book.

Enchanted by its beauty, I photographed it and sent the image to my friend Don Dennis, creator of Living Tree Orchid Essences on the Isle of Gigha in Scotland.

Even though I had used flower remedies in my practice for 22 years, I had never created one myself.

Don encouraged me to make an essence of this exquisite specimen.

Subsequently, I donated the essence of Paphiopedilum Haynaldianum to Living Tree Orchid Essences. You can order it for yourself by visiting www.healingorchids.com.

Flower essences are natural healing remedies that clear the mental, emotional and spiritual underpinnings of all illness.

I created this vibrational remedy using a non-cutting method that preserved its vivacious five blooms.

After meditating on its benefits, I received the guidance that I was to call it Reverence.

Someone once asked me what I thought was the most powerful natural healing remedies of all.

Without missing a beat, I answered, "Flower remedies!"

And without a doubt, orchid essences are the most powerful of all the flower essences because Orchidaceae are the most evolved flowers on the face of the earth and summon in the highest healing vibrations.

The Paphiopedilum Haynaldianum essence enables us to receive the beauty and wonder of all of creation.

As we heal depression, we move along a spectrum from tragedy, despair and discouragement to reverence.

We come to an acute awareness that we humans are uplifted and constantly supported by all of nature -- even when we aren't paying much attention.

If there could be only one word that accurately describes this consciousness, it would be "wow."

The orchids shine if only we take the time to look.

In alternative holistic medicine, there is a concept called the doctrine of signatures. The idea is that the flower or plant looks like the tissue, organ or disease for which it is most remedial.

You can decide for yourself what this Paphiopedilum Haynaldianum reminds you of.

But one thing I know for certain, you can either take the vibrational remedy itself - putting three drops on the acupuncture point under your tongue - or gaze upon the photograph of the orchid from which it was made.

Either one will lift up your spirit and begin to shift your perception.

It is my prayer and I believe the blessed intention of this orchid that you gaze upon this picture and begin to perceive the beauty and wonder of your own life.

Reverence.

Wow.

May this orchid bless you as much as it has blessed me.

What is HEALING?

Awaken Your
Intuitive Power for
Health and Happiness

CATHERINE
CARRIGAN

About *What Is Healing? Awaken Your Intuitive Power for Health and Happiness*

In this book, you will:

- Learn how unconditional love can awaken your intuitive gifts.
- Reveal how to open your heart to access your highest intelligence.
- Uncover how to communicate with your angels and spiritual guides.
- Awaken your own psychic abilities.
- Identify the key aspects of a medical intuitive reading.
- Discern how addiction to staying sick can keep you from healing.
- Reveal the blessing behind a mental or physical breakdown.
- Grasp the four key difficulties that lead to health problems.
- Empower your own spiritual growth.

About *Unlimited Energy Now*

Discover the secrets of how you can experience unlimited energy *now:*

- Learn how to operate your body at its very best.
- Master your own energy system.
- Resolve the emotions that drain you.
- Connect to your highest intelligence.
- Inspire yourself to connect more deeply to your infinite, eternal and unwavering support from your soul.

Made in the USA
Charleston, SC
09 September 2016